AN AMERICAN

AMONG

THE ORIENTALS.

AN AMERICAN

AMONG

THE ORIENTALS:

INCLUDING AN

AUDIENCE WITH THE SULTAN,

AND A VISIT TO THE

INTERIOR OF A TURKISH HAREM.

BY

JAMES E. P. BOULDEN, M.D.

PHILADELPHIA:
LINDSAY & BLAKISTON.
1855.

C. SHERMAN & SON, PRINTERS.

PREFACE.

THE novel characteristics of the Turks; their singular observances and beliefs; and the attitude in which they now stand before the world, owing to the complicated condition of the Russo-Greek question, involving, as it has, in a bloody struggle, not only Turkey and Russia, but the great Western powers of Europe, render authentic accounts of their manners and customs peculiarly interesting. A simple, unadorned, but truthful narration of what came under the author's observation during a few months' sojourn at Constantinople, is all that he has aimed at in the unpretending volume now modestly submitted to the public.

BALTIMORE, April 30, 1855.

CONTENTS.

CHAPTER I.

CHAPTER II.

CHAPTER III.

CHAPTER IV.

CHAPTER V.

CHAPTER VI.

CHAPTER VII.

CHAPTER VIII.

CHAPTER IX.

CHAPTER X.

CHAPTER XI.

CHAPTER XII.

CHAPTER XIII.

CHAPTER XIV.

CHAPTER XV.

CHAPTER XVI.

CHAPTER XVII.

CHAPTER XVIII.

CHAPTER XIX.

CHAPTER XX.

CHAPTER XXI.

CHAPTER XXII.

CHAPTER XXIII.

CHAPTER XXIV.

CHAPTER XXV.

CHAPTER XXVI.

TURKISH WEDDING.

CHAPTER XXVII.

CHAPTER XXVIII.

HOMEWARD BOUND.

AN AMERICAN AMONG THE ORIENTALS.

CHAPTER I.

Outward Bound—Triumph of Steam—Yankee go-a-headiveness—Fairly off—Glowing Fancies *versus* Sea-sickness—Recovery—Ludicrous Effects of the Ship's Motion.

WE live in a steam-propelling age. The waters of every sea and river, from whose margins barbaric darkness has vanished before the glorious light of human progress and civilization, are furrowed by the revolving wheel of the steam-driven vessel. Old ocean is crossed in a trice, and the voyager who, ten days previously, was threading Broadway and admiring the expanding greatness of our metropolitan city, is now gazing from the dome of St. Paul's upon London's world of brick, tile, and humanity. As in the accomplishment of almost every *other* object, so in the achievements and accompaniments of *steam* does Yankee go-a-headiveness carry off the palm from all competitors; and as no other nation can compare with us in regard to the number, vastness, comfort, magnificence, and *speed* of our noble floating palaces that ply the Hudson, the Ohio, the Mississippi, or push boldly out to the most distant seas, neither does any other people by the aid of said agents hurry into eternity so fast as we. Is it that we are such a decidedly fast nation that, not content with the ordinary rapid progression that forms a daily characteristic of our American life, we must have some speedy, high-pressure mode of exit from existence, the natural process of life's ebbing to a close being too *slow* and *tame* for *us?*

Seriously speaking, however, let us trust that ere long the rapid transits from one section to another of our extensive country will be attended by more complete guarantees of safety than at present; that legislative interference will check that unpardonable carelessness that has recently caused so many calamitous results. But it is not upon the *high seas*, as it is upon our inland waters, that, in an American steamer, we need feel any peculiar apprehension of suddenly soaring aloft, becoming charred, or meeting with a watery grave; and with the comfortable assurance of safety and almost certainly that in less than a fortnight we will be mingling in Old World scenes, let us, during the pleasant month of May, step on board the Baltic on the eve of her departure across the North Atlantic.

The last earnest grasp of the hands and the fond pressure of parting friends are over. The booming cannon and the plaudits of the assembled multitude announce that we are fairly off, and ere the lapse of but a few hours Castle Garden, Governor's, and Staten Islands, are between us and our place of embarkation. Before night has enveloped us in its dark shades we are probably careering over Atlantic's waves, and the receding shores of America have vanished behind the swelling waters. Now, having bid our native land "good night," and experienced that feeling of isolation that comes over one who, for the *first* time, is at sea, we retire to our berth to indulge in bright fancies of Europe's splendors or dream of "the friends we left behind us." Vain hope! Happy dreams and glowing fancies bless us not, but in *lieu* of them, prostrating every mental and physical energy, are all the nauseating effects of the ship's unsteady motion. A sleepless, restless night is passed. The morning dawns, yet brings us not relief. What would we *not* give, if we could only stay that horrid motion, and indulge in the briefest quietude! Food, that on land would be *delicious*, is indignantly rejected. At length, tired of confinement in a narrow berth, we venture upon deck; but, no sooner have we attained the ship's side and looked out upon the bright expanse of waters, than a sickly, deadly feeling, created by those majestic waves, *otherwise so much admired*, comes upon us; a feeling that no pen can describe, horrible to the last degree. Our head aches violently; our stomach, with all its contents, and these lend a bitter taste indeed to the tongue, appears to be crowding up into our throat and seeking an exit, which every motion of the vessel creates in us a longing desire to afford it, but without avail. We reel, the ship's unsteady motion unbalances us; we totter against and seize hold of any object that happens to be nearest; wish we had never been so foolish as to leave the firm earth, vow we never will again; look for sympathy in the face of some fellow-passenger, but find it not, for perchance he is in the same plight as ourselves; are about to give up in despair, and abandon ourselves to our sad fate, when one tremendous, but friendly lurch, produces a feeling that cannot be resisted, and with one mighty heave we dislodge our bilious accumulations, and our New York dinner of the previous day, together into the gulping waves, and thus find temporary relief.

Now, for the first time, we begin to take an interest in what is transpiring around us. We actually, though suffering so much a short time before, find ourselves amused by the queer antics which that motion, which made us sick, causes the passengers to perform. One man, thrown off his dignity and his feet simultaneously, suddenly discovers himself (for a *very* brief time, however) in a lady's lap; a couple promenading the deck are jostled violently and unceremoniously together, at the expense of each other's ribs. A walk is suddenly accelerated by the ship's *descending* motion, or retarded by its uprising. At the *table*, wine intended for the *lips* is precipitated over the *breast*, ingloriously marring that splendid sentiment, that we were about to put forth, when proposing the health of the ladies near us.

CHAPTER II.

Meditative Pleasures of Ocean Life—Resources to Kill Time on board—The Auctioneer—Betting on the Ship's Speed—The Sailor Relieved.

GRADUALLY, as time flies and the ship speeds on, we become accustomed to its every motion. We have at length thoroughly recovered from our sea-sickness. Now we feel like new beings; there is a sensation of buoyancy, of elasticity about us that we never felt before; we actually rejoice that we have been sick, so charming is the recovery from it.

Now that we have experienced all the *disagreeabilities*, we can the more keenly relish the *pleasures* of an ocean life. These are afforded those who love to gaze upon the grand and beautiful in nature, to view the rolling billows chasing and o'erleaping each other to the horizon's verge, now sparkling with the sun's noontide effulgence, or anon lit up by his more subdued rays when sinking in the western sky; or that more lovely scene afforded by the clear tranquil firmament at night—

> "Where, one by one, the living eyes of Heaven arise,
> Quick kindling o'er the face of ether
> One boundless blaze;"

and night's bright queen sheds down her softest light upon the glittering waves.

It is now, too, we are filled with "meditation deep." As we look upon the mighty expanse of water, sublime in its vastness, its profundity, and the eternal agitation of its bosom, we fully realize the wondrous power of the Great Creator of the elements and our own insignificance; the conviction comes home to us that we are in the hands of One who could speedily ride in tempest over the sea, and sink us within its lowermost depths.

Growing less serious in our contemplations, we dwell upon that partial mastery over the elements which the genius of man has achieved, that enables us to traverse mighty seas, to visit distant continents and the farthest islands, whilst yet surrounded by the comforts and luxuries of home; upon the motive power of steam, that has converted the Atlantic into a moderate sized lake, and brought the eastern and western hemispheres within ten days of each other; and a *proud*, a *happy* feeling pervades our breasts when we remember that our *own* country is inferior to *no other* in accomplishing these grand results.

But let us turn from the *meditative* to the *practical* resources adopted on board to make the time pass away agreeably.

"Going, going, gone!" What's that? It is not possible an auctioneer is on board disposing of his wares? No, not exactly disposing of merchandize, but there he is, surrounded by half the passengers, a regular New York auctioneer, well acquainted with the arts of his profession, urging upon the bystanders the value of a *number*. Humor plays upon his countenance, wit shines in all his sayings. With many a droll expression and whimsical remark he keeps his audience in a roar of laughter. Even grave D.D.'s and ladies, too, participate in the enjoyment of the scene. But what is he selling? I hear you ask. Let us explain. The ship makes every twenty-four hours a number of miles, somewhere between 250 and 320; this distance is ascertained every day at twelve o'clock. During the morning the auction takes place, each bidder having had an opportunity of judging what distance the ship ought to have made since twelve o'clock of the previous day. So the different numbers, ranging from the lowest to the highest, are sold, and that gentleman purchasing the number corresponding with the ship's speed is entitled to the pool. The sales are quite exciting and the bids spirited.

The auctioneer, and he is a genuine specimen, full of fun and frolic, begins by offering 250. He insists that that is the winning number. Last night he laid awake for several hours and heard something wrong about the machinery, in consequence of which the ship sailed miserably slow; so he contends that the holder of that number will be a lucky fellow. After considerable praising and puffing it is knocked off to John Smith for a few shillings. Then the succeeding numbers, each strongly recommended as *the* one, are disposed of, the auctioneer growing more and more racy and eloquent as he nears the *ne plus ultra.* Three hundred and twenty is offered. Here his utmost ingenuity is taxed. "Gentlemen, it is the last number, the last chance, what's bid?" "One pound." "Paugh, that's a trifle for *such* a number; why look at the sails, did you ever see canvass filled with so fine a breeze? And look at those wheels how they revolve, and tell me we are not making fourteen knots an hour. I saw the captain about an hour since, and he told me that we were making a capital run; and here, gentlemen, allow me to correct myself about being awake last night. I was under a slight mistake. Since this sale begun I have reasoned the matter with myself, and discover that it was all a dream about our going slow. The engineers assure me that the machinery worked admirably; so bid up briskly for 320; it is *the* number, and no mistake." At length, in the midst of wit and merriment, it is sold. Thus ends the auction for that day.

These sales, at first glance, appear to be a species of gambling; but when we are acquainted with the fact that one-half of the proceeds goes to the relief of the poor sailor we are not apt to condemn them.

CHAPTER III.

The Smoking-Room—Ladies' Saloon—A Home Picture—Sunday on the Ocean—Divine Service—Bishop Wainwright—Character and Manners of the Passengers.

Aft is the smoking-room. At all hours, but especially after dinner, when the number is increased, are here gathered, engaged in conversation or lost in forgetfulness amid the fumes of choice Cuba leaf, those whose stomachs are not peculiarly disposed to succumb to the combined influence of the ship's see-saw motion and the dense atmosphere of the place.

Below, in the magnificently furnished ladies' saloon, where, but for the jarring motion of machinery and an occasional lurch of the boat, one would fancy himself in one of the most splendidly adorned and comfortably arranged drawing-rooms of America, is clustered an agreeable company of ladies and gentlemen around a piano, listening to the soft strains of music; a young lady is skilfully touching the keys, mingling with their harmony her own clear voice, whose dulcet warblings, seconded by a gentleman's strong bass, form a strange and delightful contrast with the rushing element without. It is indeed a home picture, that group around the singers and the instrument; those four indulging in a social game of whist; those damask velvet cushions tempting to ease and indolence; those mirrors, large and costly, reflecting every object in the room; those domestics hurrying here and there with the most delicious fruits; the innocent prattle of children in their nurse's laps or tumbling over the floor; and that friendly social feeling pervading the assembly.

But it is *Sunday*—Sunday in the midst of the ocean! No loud and prolonged succession of church-bell peals, as on land, in a Christian country, breaks upon the stillness of the morn. One single bell, rung measuredly, reminds us that it is the Sabbath of the Lord, and summons us to His worship; and how solemn and impressive is Divine service out on that boundless waste of waters! There, gathered in the aft saloon, and with attentive ears listening to the eloquent pleadings of some such eminent divine as Dr. Wainwright, of New York,* are Christians of all

* This gentleman, then a delegate to the World's Convention,

creeds, forgetting their sectarian prejudices, kneeling down to, and singing the praises of one common Redeemer, and acknowledging His omnipotence. What place more meet for such acknowledgment? Under what circumstances could we feel ourselves more palpably in the power of God, or so readily appreciate our individual worthlessness and insignificance in contrast with His glory and might?

Having noticed some of the most prominent events that lend an interest to a sea-voyage, let us look about us and see what variety of people, character, and manners we have on board.

Here is a real Jonathan, from "away down East," who saunters about in truly republican style, whistling some such air as "Hail Columbia," and "willing to bet any amount" that America is ahead of "all creation" in *anything* you can start; *there* is a warm-blooded Southerner from the cotton country, on his way to lands where, though slavery exist not in *form*, yet doth it in *principle*. Walking hurriedly up and down the deck, ready for a "*bolt*" upon the first sound of the dinner gong, are a couple of young Englishmen, who have been making a tour through

was a fellow-passenger of the writer, on board the Baltic, in May of '52.

the States, and are now returning, after a year's absence from their own country, with many a preconceived notion and prejudice in reference to *ours* dispelled by observation; venerable divines are there, visiting the *old* as ecclesiastic representatives of the *new* world; book-writers *too* are on board, taking notes, with the view some day of edifying the world with the results of their observation. Here and there are men or women whose feeble motions and pallid countenances convince us that they are seeking, in the briny air, the tumultuous action of the sea, a change of scene, &c., that precious boon, *good health;* men whose heads are covered with the frosts of age are now for the first time venturing over the great deep; middle-aged and youth, the latter fresh from the trammels of collegiate life and glowing with the enthusiasm of travel; the miss not yet emerged from her teens, ardent and romantic, her mind filled with bright anticipations of those lands of beauty and of song that have long impressed themselves upon the dreams of her youth, and upon which, ere long, she hopes to gaze and tread; the diplomat, after a brief visit to his friends in America, returning to his honorable post at a foreign court; merchants on their way to purchase the fabrics of Western Europe, which a goodly portion of our fellow-citizens deem superior to our own, not *always* because they have a firmer texture or more perfect finish, but oft, I ween, on account of its being supposed that the productions of a *foreign* loom must *necessarily* surpass *our own;* gentlemen retired from the busy scenes of money-making life, now spending their time and their means for the relaxation, entertainment, and information afforded by travel; people speaking various languages, the loquacious Frenchman, the gesticulating Spaniard, the meerschaum-smoking, beer-drinking German, and even the short-cropped Russian, are all there, mingling in social harmony like one large family. Whatever may be their individual tastes, their personal, sectional, or national prejudices, these are all merged into a desire to please and to be pleased; no angry words are spoken, no unpleasant scenes are witnessed; all act like persons moving on to the harmonious accomplishment of one grand purpose.

CHAPTER IV.

Nearing Land—Anxiety increases to reach it—"Fastinet Light"—Coast of Ireland—St. George's Channel—The Last Dinner—Wine and Speeches—A Golden Sunset—Arrive at Liverpool.

At length we near the shores of Europe, and our breasts heave with new delight that our voyage, pleasant as it has been, is about to terminate; that we are soon once more to set our foot upon something stable, our eyes on aught else beside the tossing wave.

We think not so much of land when out but a few days; we feel that a certain time *must* elapse before we can reach the shore for which we are destined, and with a commendable philosophy divert our minds with whatever is transpiring around us; but, when conscious that the land toward which we are steering is not far distant, how anxious we become, how we long for a glance of it, how we stretch our vision and elevate the captain's spy-glass to discern the first faint outlines on the distant horizon! And then the interval between the first cheerful glimpse of, and our arrival at, it, appears longer than any day we have spent on the Atlantic; the shores actually appear to retreat, and we feel as if we never will reach them. But in the course of time the "Fastinet Light," standing out in majestic relief upon an isolated rock, the ocean dashing in restless breakers around it, whilst *it* stands high and firm, as if in proud defiance of the elements, is passed. Soon, upon the verge of a hill four hundred and fifty feet above high water, is perceived Cape Clear lighthouse, whilst deep valley and high hill follow each other in quick succession, almost every revolution of the wheels developing new objects along the rock-bound coast of Ireland, whose general aspect, though dreary *else*, yet gladdens *now* the *voyager's* weary vision, and enables him to perceive, in the distant hills crowned with manor residences and surrounded by parks, the white-crested waves dashing against the rocky shore, the Irish craft ploughing the waves, with light fleecy clouds hovering over all, a beautiful and pleasant picture.

And now the great ocean is crossed. We are in St. George's Channel, and with bounding hearts view every object on land and water that denotes our near approach to port. We go below and partake of our *last* dinner. This occasion, we find, affords a fine opportunity for the display of eloquence. The wine *that* day is furnished by the captain. The noble qualities, social and seaman-like, of that gentleman, are spoken of in the most laudatory terms; reference is had to the prosperous voyage that is about to terminate, to the intercommunication existing between the two enlightened countries of England and America, produced mainly through the medium of the magnificent steamers of the respective countries; an intercourse calculated not only to promote *their* interests and prosperity, but to produce a social and political advantageous effect on countries less favored with liberal and beneficent institutions; allusion is made to the great harmony existing between the passengers during the whole voyage, &c.

Everything passes off very agreeably at the table, and after a pretty heavy imbibition of champagne, the passengers all once more assemble upon deck. It is their last evening on board; the sunset is beautiful in the extreme; the golden orb goes down in radiant splendor behind the Irish hills, casting a halo of glory over land and sea; soon a lovely crescent moon, with bright stars for her companions, lights up the clear blue vault of heaven. That night we are rocked to sleep by St. George's billows, and the following morning, greeted by the American flags in the Mersey, arrive at Liverpool.

We are taken to shore in a small steamer, into which we all crowd, the gentlemen standing. Just as we are moving off, we give three hearty cheers for the gallant officers and noble ship that have brought us so safely over the Atlantic; and with no slight feeling of regret do we part with either, or entertain the thought that we are nearing the point of separation from many agreeable acquaintances whom we have met on board, and whom perchance we may never see again. In a few minutes we effect a landing, and are soon comfortably accommodated at the "Adelphi," in Liverpool.

CHAPTER V.

Western Europe — The Orient — Embark on board an Austrian Steamer—Politeness of the Captain—His friendliness towards America—Approach the "City of the Sultan"—Accident—Ineffable Beauty—Constantinople—Seraglio Point—The Golden Horn —Amphitheatre of Beauty.

WESTERN EUROPE is so thoroughly described by the modern tourist that we deem it superfluous to tire the patience of the reader by dwelling on the scenes we witnessed whilst traversing England, France, Italy, Switzerland, &c. The quaint old cities, and the noble and venerable palaces and cathedrals of the continent, are almost as familiar to the general reader as if he had wandered through their historic streets, gorgeous apartments, and sacred aisles.

Supposing that you, kind reader, are as anxious, as were we, to reach that portion of the world, the very reference to which stirs up romantic and poetical emotions, the beauteous Orient, with its luxurious clime, the novel and picturesque manners and costumes of its people, its fair and lovely daughters, &c., we invite you to embark with us at Trieste, in an Austrian steamer, for Constantinople.

The captain of the "Asia" was extremly polite to us during the whole of our very pleasant voyage, from Trieste to Constantinople; which rather surprised us, as we were under the impression that from the Austrians we would, being Americans, of that country which had offered so safe a shelter to their most dangerous foe, meet with nought but rudeness and incivility.

Captain Poiret made frequent mention of America, and in the most friendly terms. He referred to the rapid advancement of the arts and sciences in our country, spoke of the American inventive genius, of the superiority of our ships and steamers. He appeared to honor the names of Washington, Franklin, and Fulton.

Upon my telling him that we *rather* went ahead of *all creation* in the way of *steaming*, he said, "Yes, you go ahead most *too* fast, sometimes the boiler bursts, you go *up*, and then,—*adieu!*" He had heard something about certain accidents which *occasionally* occur on our Western waters.

As a general thing, the captains of European

steamers are very cautious. They never race, and an explosion is a very rare event with them.

As we sailed over the placid waters of the Marmora, and approached the "City of the Sultan," I was all impatience to see that famous place, that had so long been a bright and beauteous picture in my imagination. Long before "old Sol" had reddened the east, on the morn that we anticipated catching a glimpse of the distant city, I hurried on deck, expecting to see its manifold beauties unfolded in all their glory; but alas! for the fallacy of human hopes, I was doomed to disappointment—instead of the city, with its populous suburbs, a broad expanse of water, only bounded by the horizon, was all that greeted my vision.

An accident occurred during the night, which so implicated the boat's machinery, that we had to be towed up to the city by a Turkish and English steamer; and so slowly did we advance, that the sun had passed the zenith ere we came in sight of old Stambool. It was two o'clock, P. M., when its mosques, its towering minarets and mournful cypress trees, appeared in the distance; and how inadequate to the task of describing the scene that then presented itself do I feel!

All the glowing fancies which had, for half my lifetime, filled my mind, of oriental splendor and magnificence, as so graphically portrayed in the "Arabian Nights," appeared to be realized. Millions of reams of paper and oceans of ink have been consumed, and the human language almost exhausted in faint endeavors to describe the glorious and magnificent picture afforded by the approach, from the Sea of Marmora, to Constantinople. To the traveller from the Western world the scene is so new and peculiar, so essentially different from anything he has ever before witnessed, so novel and oriental withal, as to appear more like a strangely beautiful dream, which the waking senses will dissipate, than a palpable reality. He has dwelt upon the beauty and grandeur of the French metropolis; with alternate awe and admiration looked down from the giddy heights of the Alpine passes; or feasted his eyes upon the ravishing loveliness of Switzerland's matchless lakes and valleys; the "City of the Sea" has charmed his vision, the beautiful Venice itself, where the tranquil waters of the Adriatic lave the marble steps of a thousand palaces, and where there is all of tradition and all of glory in the associations of the past to give a zest to the enjoyment of the beauteous present; yet have all these failed to awaken within him so great admiration as the scene now before him. Proudly there, upon its seven hills, stands Constantinople; its gilded mosques and minarets flashing back, with a golden hue, the sun's resplendent rays. Seraglio Point looks like a miniature Paradise, with its many domes so charmingly commingled with the cypress, and forms in itself a complete Eastern picture of grace and loveliness.

When we rounded Seraglio Point, we found ourselves within an amphitheatre of beauty. The city, its suburbs both on the European and Asiatic shores; the Bosphorus lined with gardens and palaces; the Golden Horn filled with ships from whose masts floated the flags of all nations; the large war-ships of the Sultan, one or two of which carry one hundred and forty guns; the thousands of slim and graceful caiques that shot about in every direction over the surface of the water, filled with grave Turks, robed in the fanciful and flowing garments of the East—all combined to make up this matchless picture.

CHAPTER VI.

At Anchor—Sleeping on Deck—A Confused Scene—A Modern Babel—Pera—Conflagrations—Means of extinguishing them—Turkish *versus* American Firemen—A Singular Mode of showing the Dissatisfaction of the People.

At length the rattling chain announced the sinking of the anchor, and we came to a standstill in the harbor. In connection with the scene which then ensued, I would remark that the Turk, be he a Pasha, or one of the lowest subjects of the realm, scarcely ever goes below in a ship. He prefers spreading his bed upon the open deck, where he can enjoy the fresh breezes of Heaven.

One-half of our aft deck, it being separated by a temporary partition from the other half, or first class passenger part, was completely covered with mattresses, over which were strewn men, women, and children, reclining at night, and squatting *à la Turque* through the day.

When we had fairly stopped, there was a general

confusion; our oriental passengers were the chief actors in the scene; there was a grand resurrection of bodies that had been in a semi-recumbent position for four or five days and nights; an universal folding up and arranging of beds and bedding; a squabbling among the children; chattering among the women; much talk and smoke among the men; whilst all around the steamer were hovering caiques, filled with Turks, Greeks, Armenians, &c., running in contact with each other, quarrelling, crying out to the passengers, shrieking in all languages; thus rendering the scene a perfect Babel.

In an hour or two we found ourselves deserted by most of the caiques and passengers, leaving us surrounded by soliciting hotel agents, whom we soon despatched, as we had pretty well learned, during our travels on the continent, how to proceed in quest of quarters without the assistance of a dozen advisers.

That night we were comfortably fixed in Pera, which is mostly inhabited by Franks; and, being separated from Constantinople by the Golden Horn, is quite a distinct city. The houses of this place are mostly large, and of late years have been built of stone, to prevent the fearful ravages so frequently made there by fires.

They are generally constructed in the European style and afford a striking contrast with the small frame tenements of the Turks. Speaking of fires reminds me that for a month or two after our arrival in Constantinople, we were in the midst of them. I had often heard of the destructive conflagrations with which that city was afflicted, but certainly was not prepared to find them occurring so frequently as they did. Eleven large fires occurred within a few weeks, the last destroying about three thousand houses, and turning five thousand families into the streets. It looks really terrible to see the devouring element lighting up the whole heavens at night, demolishing miles of houses, and rendering so many wretched people homeless.

There are not those efficient means of extinguishing fires that we have in the United States, and the firemen of our country would be amused at the apparatus used, and the inducements which set the firemen to work. The engine is so small that it can be worked by four men. It is carried on their shoulders and is supplied with water by hamals or porters who convey it in leathern vessels strapped on their backs.

The firemen will not stir an inch towards rescuing

a house until they have received a *backshish* or payment in money. What a contrast this affords with the conduct of those gallant firemen of our cities who so heroically peril life and limb, for no compensation, to save the property of their fellow-citizens?

How often have I wished, when the devouring element was soaring triumphantly, that an *American* engine, worked by *American* firemen, was present to arrest its progress. However, the streets are too narrow for any other apparatus to be taken through them than that now in use, and I must do the Turkish firemen the justice to say that when they *once* get to work they go at it like tigers, and as their engines, small as they are, can throw a stream a hundred feet, they serve, in connection with the general practice of tearing down houses in the vicinity of the fire, as assistants at least.

In former times, whenever the people desired to evince their dissatisfaction with the Government, they fired the city night after night until a change of the Ministry took place. The Sultan, knowing the *cause* of these incendiary acts, and fearing the great impoverishment they were calculated to produce among his subjects, responded to their wishes, and changed his ministers.

This is supposed to have been the case whilst we were at Constantinople, as the ministers who were in power when we first arrived, were odious in the eyes of the people, fires followed each other in quick succession, but a ministerial change taking place, they were comparatively rare afterwards.

CHAPTER VII.

A Ride through Constantinople on Horseback—People of all Nations and Costumes—Turks, Greeks, Jews, Moors, Arabs, Persians, &c.—Turkish and Armenian Women—The *Ferigee* and *Yashmak*—*Hamals*, Donkeys, and Horses—Dogs of Constantinople and Pera—Their Peculiarities.

A FEW days after our arrival, I traversed the principal thoroughfares of Constantinople on horseback, and really the interesting and diversified objects that attracted my attention were well worth the trouble and risk of such a ride.

People of all nations, clad in their respective costumes, were to be seen: the grave and slowly-moving Turks, or their more energetic neighbors, the Armenians (the latter, presenting pretty much the same appearance on the *street*, as the former) waddling along in their full breeches, their loose, blue jackets, heavily embroidered with gold and silk, below which, stuck in rich Cashmere scarfs appeared certain formidable fire-arms and Damascus blades, which caused me instinctively to give their wearers plenty of room to pass; their heads surmounted by large turbans, or the red fez of modern times, their venerable beards falling over their breasts; tall Greeks, with braided jackets, vests, and leggings, snow-white and ample skirts, rich Persian sashes encircling their narrow waists, jaunty caps, &c.; wily Jews, with their long and flowing garments; dark Moors and Arabs, attired in the wild costumes peculiar to the wandering and tent-dwelling life of the desert; darkly clothed Persians, with their conspicuous, towering, sharp-pointed hats, and perhaps a pile of costly shawls, of their own country, or Cashmere thrown over their shoulders; fur-clad Georgians, Circassians, and Russians; whilst, here and there, appeared a fat Pasha on horseback, with a dozen attendants pursuing him on foot; or, a representative of civilized Europe, whose tall, awkward hat, scant coat, and "tights," rendered him about as odd-looking a biped as any among this motley group: these among the men.

Among the women, groups of whom crowded the streets, there was not so great a variety of costumes.

They all wore *ferigees* or long full garments somewhat resembling a priest's robe, composed of various materials and brightly colored. These extended from their necks to their feet, and were held up in front with one hand to keep them from trailing. The head and all the face, saving the eyes, were covered with the *yashmak* or Turkish veil; which is composed of a white and delicately fine muslin, and is kept perfectly clean and snow-like. On their feet were yellow boots, over which they wore slippers with no heels, in which they half walked, half slid, from place to place.

The *ferigee* and *yashmak* impart a very singular and sepulchral appearance to the Turkish women, making them look as though they had just arisen from beneath the marble slabs that adorn their own cypress-shaded cemeteries.

Between the *yashmak's* white folds I discerned many a pair of large, brilliant eyes, black, long-lashed and voluptuous; and as Franks particularly attract the attention of the Turkish women, I had a fine opportunity of observing their rolling orbs.

Some of the Armenian women wear such thin *yashmaks* that their features can be discerned through the delicate material. Many of the Armenian women in the suburbs of Constantinople do not wear the veil at all, but their fear of the Turks prevents those residing in the city from dispensing with it. Even the *Turkish* women, *especially those who think themselves handsome*, appear to be disposed to rid themselves of an article which so effectually screens their beauty from the admiring gaze of the passer-by.

Among the other objects that claimed my attention were the immense number of donkeys, hundreds of which were toiling through the streets under burdens that appeared calculated to sink them to the ground. Then there were the *hamals*, or porters, carrying loads on *their* backs equal to the *united* weight of the donkey and his burden; and to complete the picture, wolfish-looking dogs were prowling about, or lazily lying in the streets, undisturbed by all these moving scenes, save when they felt the pressure of a horse's foot, or that of some unwary pedestrian, on their tails.

As the streets of Turkish cities are too narrow for heavy vehicles all ponderous articles have necessarily to be carried on the backs of *hamals*, horses, or mules. Even all heavy building materials, lumber, stone, and bricks, are transported by these means, great distances and up steep ascents.

I have referred to the *risk* of navigating through such a living channel on horseback, not because the

Turks are, as is generally thought, a ferocious people, but on account of the crowd and confusion, the narrowness of the streets, and the fact that you may, in consequence thereof, excite the ire of *some* one, you do not know whom (he may be a *Bedouin* or *worse*), by running your horse against him; or you may bring down the vengeance of some pious Mussulman upon you on account of your horse's hoofs setting one of his canine neighbors to howling.

Everybody has heard of the dogs of Constantinople; the city swarms with them. They have no owners, but make their beds in the middle of the public thoroughfares, or the commons, and depend for their food upon Moslem charity.

They have a wolfish, half-famished look, and are divided into gangs, each gang occupying a particular quarter of the city, and promptly repelling any trespassing dogs that venture on its premises. As it is an injunction of the Koran to be merciful to all animals, the dog scarcely ever receives any blows from a Turk; and to perceive that the Turks are obedient to Mahomet's precepts it is only necessary to witness the difference in the actions of a dog of Constantinople and one of Pera, when a club is elevated to strike him. The *latter*, under such circumstances, with that instinctive dread, caused by the recollection of certain disagreeable impressions which have been made upon him at sundry times, by the denizens of "Infidel Hill," flies off at a tangent with a howl; with the *former*, mere *threats* are of no avail; having been accustomed to the largest liberty from his puppyhood, to lay where, and bark when, he pleases, and being moreover possessed of a true oriental indolence, *actual blows*, horse's heels, or carriage-wheels, are the only things that will arouse him from his lethargy.

CHAPTER VIII.

Ramazan—Its Rigid Observance—Evening Scenes and Enjoyments —Cafés—The Turk's Fondness for the Pipe—The Oriental's Inclination to Seek for Enjoyment amid the Abodes of the Dead—Separation of the Sexes—The Harem—The Salamnik—Luxurious Enjoyments of the Females.

It was during the Holy Month Ramazan that we arrived at Constantinople. This month Mahomet set apart for fasting and self-denial. His followers are then prohibited (from three o'clock in the morning until sundown), from eating, drinking, or even *smoking*, abstinence from the latter enjoyment being the sorest trial of all.

On account of the way in which time is reckoned among the Mahomedans, the Ramazan in the course of years runs through every season, and that year, (1852) occurring in midsummer, its strict observance was peculiarly trying; still, such is the veneration of the Turk for the commands of the prophet of Mecca, that, amidst all his toil, under the burning rays of an Eastern sun, he will take, in the specified time, no nourishment; and though, as he labors up the steep heights of Pera and Constantinople, his eye rests, almost every moment, upon a marble fountain with its clear gushing water, yet no cooling draught refreshes his fevered thirst.

The city towards evening presents a far different picture from that witnessed through the day. When the lengthening shadows intimate the almost finished course of the sun, many a Moslem eye is regarding his diminishing rays with peculiar interest. The cafés, as yet deserted, are being swept, seats are being arranged in front of them for the expected guests, pipes are being prepared, coffee warmed, and sherbet cooled. Soon the crowd collects, and the seats of the cafés are occupied by long-bearded Turks, before whom are placed *nargalas*, with their long tubes gracefully winding over them, their cut glass and decanter-formed bodies half filled with rose-water—and their perforated earthen bowls holding the grateful tobacco.

At length the booming cannon from a neighboring fortress announces the setting of the sun; almost simultaneously with which a thousand curling eddies of smoke convince the passer-by that the long agony is over, and that the Moslem devotee is indulging in bright reveries of Paradise, and luxuriates in a blissful oblivion to all surrounding objects, amid the care-dispelling fumes of his pipe.

After smoking for awhile, he sips strong coffee out of diminutive cups, which are handed around generally by Greek attendants. The drinking of this beverage *always succeeds* the use of the pipe ; after which sherbet, cooled by snow from Olympus, is partaken of; then follows a promiscuous diet.

The reader will perceive, from what we have just written, that, though the Turk has denied himself both food and drink for about fifteen hours, yet his first consideration after the expiration of the prescribed period of abstinence, is the *everlasting pipe.*

As the sun, viewed from Constantinople, sets behind Olympus, on the evening of the closing day of *Ramazan,* a Turk is stationed on that classic mount to give the earliest intimation to the self-sacrificing, but now rejoicing, Mahomedans, that the last sun of the Holy Month has set.

We have referred to the cafés ; some of these are patronized almost exclusively by Turks, others by a mixture of Turks, Armenians, and other orientals, whilst others still are frequented principally by Franks.

The best cafés are those in the vicinity of the cemetery, both within and without the city. There appears to be a *penchant* in the East to seek for pleasure and enjoyment amid the gloomy abodes of the dead; and, with many a curiously wrought tombstone rising up to the view all around them, upon which, engraven in gilded letters, are inscriptions recording the virtues of some one who has gone to his long account, or admonishing the looker-on of the uncertainty of this life, and the preparations necessary to the enjoyment of a perfect one in Paradise, are, every evening, seated a merry throng, smoking, chatting, drinking, and listening to the soft strains of Italian music, or the less refined but stranger tones of a Turkish band.

Women do not make their appearance at a *Turkish* café. In fact, Turkish females do not, on any occasion, out of doors, mingle with the men. Even when the denizens of Constantinople, in order to escape the heat of the city, resort to some of the beautiful valleys opening into the Bosphorus, to spend the day in pic-nic style, the two sexes do not associate with each other, but have separate places to ramble about in or spread their mats.

It would be an extremely dangerous experiment for

a Turkish gentleman to walk, stand, or converse with a Turkish lady in any *public* place. The chances are that he would be seized by a *cavasse*, or public officer, and be compelled to suffer some kind of penalty for his temerity; and that too even if the woman be his *own wife*.

The reason is obvious. How can he *prove* that she is *his* wife,—she may be any other man's. The *ferigee* and *yashmak* entirely conceal her, with the exception of the eyes; these resemble a *thousand* pair; she will not presume to expose her face; her testimony, *under the circumstances*, is not taken; so what is the bewildered gallant or husband to do but suffer the consequences of his indiscretion?

It is not only out of doors where the two sexes are separated. Even at home they occupy distinct and separate apartments. The portion of the house occupied by the man is called the *salamnik*, and that part in which the wife or wives live is termed the *harem*.

The windows of the *harem* are closely latticed to prevent its inmates from being observed by outsiders. No male infidel vision ever penetrates into those sacred recesses where, reclining luxuriously upon rich, gold-embroidered, cloth divans, the air glowing with Arabia's sweetest perfumes, surrounded by their female attendants, who hearken to their every sigh, and hurriedly obey their every wish, now refreshing them with snow-cooled sherbet, and anon lulling their senses with soft voluptuous music, these houris while away the time in blissful indolence.

CHAPTER IX.

Wives and Slaves—Number of former allowed by the Koran—Reason why Turks generally have but one Wife—Turkish Wife's Extravagance—Valleys of the "Sweet Waters of Europe and of Asia"—Picturesque Scenes—Ox Arabas—Female costume—Arabian Jugglers—Amusements of the Men—Dashing Steeds.

SOME of the wealthy Turks have two or three wives, besides several slaves, who are generally the fairest women of Georgia and Circassia; as a *general* thing, however, they have but *one* wife, though the Koran allows them *four*.

The Sultan *himself* has no more than this last number, but at the same time he has between two and three hundred of the most lovely female *slaves*.

The common impression among us is that the Turks can have as many wives as they please, or can support; this is an erroneous idea, as they can never transcend the number specified in the Koran.

The reason that the privilege, extended to them by Mahomet, of having more than *one* wife, is not more frequently availed of by the Turks, is attributable to its *expensiveness.*

It is no trifling matter to support *one* wife, to keep around her the necessary attendants, to supply her with diamonds, which she requires the greatest abundance of to deck herself or children with; to furnish her with bazaar money, which is expended for the fine silks of Persia, jewelled slippers, or cashmere shawls; all of which appear to be the indispensable requisites of a Turkish wife. When these expenses are threatened to be doubled or trebled, it is not a matter of any great surprise that the Turk remains satisfied with one partner.

The beautiful valleys to which I have incidentally referred, where the residents of Constantinople have their *keffs* or pic-nics, are, on those occasions, most excellent places to observe the Turkish women.

The principal resorts are the valleys of the Sweet Waters of Asia and of Europe. These, every Friday, (the Turkish Sabbath), present the most animated and diversified appearance that can be conceived of.

On the margin of a small clear stream that meanders through the valley, and under the shade of overhanging trees, may be seen spread, hundreds of richly worked Persian mats; upon which are seated, in picturesque groups, the Turkish women, their black busy eyes peering out between the folds of *yashmaks*, whose whiteness is of virgin purity.

Gaily painted and gilded *arabas*, drawn by oxen, are slowly moving along, containing women, reclining on cushions, who, like their friends on the bank, are chattering, looking eagerly around upon the crowd, especially scrutinizing the Frank whom curiosity has attracted to their vicinity, and surveying themselves in small mirrors, which they carry with them on such occasions. Here and there are children scampering about or walking with all the dignity of men and women, their little bodies almost covered with diamonds and other precious gems.

It is only on the little *girls* that we could see the costume which the *ferigee* and *yashmak* hid on the adults; the loose pantaloons descending below a long, full skirt, open in front, and festooned up at the side; their heads being ornamented with diamonds, &c.

Toward the lower part of the valley, an Arabian juggler has collected around him a crowd of astonished females, who evince their appreciation of his wonderful tricks by shrill bursts of laughter, and an increased magnitude of their already amply large eyes.

Still farther down, near the Bosphorus, are gathered

the men; the faithful representation of whose various costumes, positions, &c., would defy the most adroit brush that ever made the canvas glow with life, and futile would be any attempt of my feeble pen to delineate them. Turks, Armenians, Greeks, Jews, Arabs, and Albanians, are there gathered; clad in the gaudy costumes of their respective countries, standing, walking, squatting *à la Turque*, smoking, drinking coffee and sherbet; and all, save the profoundly grave Turks, breaking out into the most immoderate fits of laughter at the surprising feats and antics of a couple of Arab wizards, who, with wild looks and actions, and in wilder guttural tones, are astonishing their senses.

In the extreme upper portion of the "Valley of the Sweet Waters of Asia," is a large area, over whose level and grass-covered surface, during the weekly jollifications, dash richly caparisoned horses, which, with their well-conditioned and richly clothed riders, pursued on foot by armed attendants, add greatly to the interest of the general scene.

CHAPTER X.

An Audience with Sultan Abdul Medjid—Rowed by American Sailors—The Bosphorus—Boat of the American Legation—Emotions on beholding the Flag of our Native Land—Reach the Sultan's Palace—Reception-Room—Our Appearance—Pipe-Bearers—Mode of Presenting the Pipe—Magnificent Amber and Jewelled Mouth-pieces—Their Abundance—Turkish Tobacco—Former Smoking Customs—Sarfs—Coffee—Enter the Palace—An Exhibition of our Veneration for the "Shadow of God on Earth"—The Sultan's "Pages."

WHILST we were at Constantinople, the Hon. George P. Marsh, United States Minister at the Sublime Porte, sailed in the United States Steamship San Jacinto, for Athens, to settle certain difficulties between Mr. King, an American Missionary, and the Greek Government.

On the occasion of his departure, he had an audience with the Sultan, who, at the time, was occupying a palace on the Asiatic shores of the Bosphorus.

Availing myself of so rare an opportunity to see *His Sublime Highness*, face to face, I became attached to the Minister's suite; and as it was *impossible* to be ushered into the Royal presence in the plain garb of a civilian, I was under the necessity of doffing it, and rigging myself *en militaire.*

Towards noon, we left the San Jacinto, John P. Brown, Esq., of the United States Legation, Captain Crabbe, and several of his officers, being of the party.

Propelled by the lusty arms of American sailors, we glided rapidly over the quiet waters of the Golden Horn and Bosphorus; now wending our way between scores of light *caiques,* that were cleaving the waters in all directions, and anon passing under the frowning batteries of the Sultan's prodigious gun-ships, that were anchored out in the stream.

Ascending the Bosphorus a couple of miles, we discerned in the distance, rounding one of those glorious promontories for which this noble channel is so famous, a large *caique,* rowed by nine *caiquejies* or boatmen, all of whom were clad in white silk shirts.

A large eagle, with expanded wings, perched upon its bow, and the star-spangled banner floating at the stern, soon convinced us that it was the boat of the American Legation.

What heartfelt emotions were awakened by the contemplation of the "Banner of the Free," waving over those foreign waters, where we were separated by seas and continents from our native land! The feelings are indeed patriotic and proud, that a true-hearted American experiences when beholding his country's flag upon a distant sea or soil. He who has never left the free shores of America, and traversed the despotic countries of the Old World, cannot realize them.

The boat had on board the United States Minister, and bending our course, as did it (as we approached each other), towards the Asiatic shore, we soon found ourselves sailing in company with the Minister, in the direction of the Sultan's palace. That reached, we landed on a marble quay, in the presence of two files of soldiery, which formed the outer guards of the palace.

We were then conducted by an officer through a court paved with marble, and, between two other rows of soldiers, into the reception-room; where, by the guidance of the master of ceremonies, we seated ourselves on the divans, which there, as in almost every Turkish house, extended around three sides of the room.

We were arranged in a line *vis-a-vis* with the German Legation, whose chief had also come to take leave of His Imperial Majesty.

On account of our number, and the style of our uniform, we made quite a formidable appearance; and when I looked on both sides of me, I felt really *proud* of the fine picture our little republican party presented at the Court of the descendant of the Ottomans.

A few minutes after we were seated, a troop of pipe-bearers filed into the room, each bearing the eternal pipe.

They approached us with measured steps and dignity, and, with one hand pressed against their hearts, with the other presented to each of us a pipe, and then retreated, with their faces directed toward us, until they were completely out of the room. This was all accomplished with the utmost precision and regularity, and though there were over a dozen of us served at the same time, our long pipes stretching out on the floor, forming stumbling-blocks to less experienced persons, and though each pipe-bearer walked *backwards*, there was no coming in contact either with each other or the pipes.

We were struck with the richness of the amber and jewelled mouth-pieces of the pipes; row after row of diamonds, rubies, sapphires, &c., made up their glittering beauty.

Lieutenant Wainwright and myself calculated the value of the mouth-pieces through which *we* smoked, and we came to the conclusion that each one could not be worth less than two thousand dollars. But some were far richer than ours, the approximate value of which I would not like to state, lest I be charged with exaggeration.

There appeared to be a profusion of these gem-sparkling pipes, for notwithstanding each of *our* party was served, the German Legation was also served with them, and we must hence conclude that there is a sufficiency on hand to supply any number of embassies that may happen to seek an interview with His Highness, on one and the same day.

The tobacco had a very delicate flavor, and I should think, on account of its pleasantness and the magnificent mouth-pieces through which it was whiffed, that the most rigidly abstemious person in the world would have been tempted to take a few puffs. Just to think of a glorious inhalation of the fumes of the finest tobacco of Turkey, through transparent amber and rings of diamonds, worth thousands of dollars!

Formerly, it was the custom, when one Turkish dignitary visited another, to have pipes brought out for him and those accompanying him as *friends;* but as this was a very expensive fashion, involving the necessity of keeping an *unlimited* number of pipes, it is now almost abandoned, and each guest or visiter, if he be a man of any consequence, takes his own pipes (borne by pipe-bearers) with him.

It is really amusing to see a Turkish grandee galloping along on horseback, with a train of attendants pursuing him on foot, conspicuous among whom are the pipe-bearers.

Of course, it is not expected of the Franks to carry the Tchibouk with them, and hence provision is always made for *them.*

After a brief enjoyment of our pipes, another relay of servants marched into the room, bearing small cups, placed in magnificent *sarfs*, the latter vying with the amber mouth-pieces in the richness of their material and adornments, and served us with the most delicious coffee, which article the Turks excel in making.

The smoking, the drinking of coffee and sherbet, and some friendly chatting in French, with the Master of Ceremonies, having been gone through with, a messenger made his appearance, announcing that His Imperial Majesty was ready to receive us.

Rising and following him, we crossed over a court, paved with gravel mosaic, and mounting the marble steps, passed into the Grand Entrance of the Palace, which was guarded on either side by Turkish soldiers. Here the *faithful* are compelled to doff their shoes, using slippers as a substitute, as it would be the height of sacrilege to mar the marble or oak-panelled floors of the Palace, wherein dwells the "Shadow of God on earth," with the heavy and soiled foot-coverings of the street.

But we infidels were spared that trouble, and planted our calf-skins or patent-leathers (*with our feet in them*), on the clean and highly polished floors of the Imperial Mansion, with such *nonchalance*, that the devout disciples of the Holy Prophet must have been wonderfully surprised at our want of veneration.

We continued on through two successive apartments, both furnished in the most regal and Eastern style; in the first of which, drawn up in a double column, were the "pages" of the Sultan, who, with their tall helmets and feathers, looked very grand and picturesque.

CHAPTER XI.

Audience with the Sultan, continued—Enter the Sultan's Apartment Turkish Salutation—Mr. Marsh's Speech—The Sultan's Reply—Description of the Sultan's Person—His Dress—Profusion of Diamonds—Inverted feet and their Cause—Abdul Medjid as compared with Mahmoud the Second—Energy of the Latter—His Reforms—Benevolence of the present Sultan—His Liberal Policy towards Christians—His want of Energy—Stagnation of the Empire—Its Cause—Unequalness of Taxation—Presentation of Mr. Brown—Backing-out Ceremonies.

On entering into the third apartment of the palace our eyes fell upon His Majesty, the Sultan, who was standing, with no one near him save the Minister of Foreign Affairs, in the remotest part of it, awaiting our approach.

We advanced to within three yards of him and then made the usual Turkish salutation, which (the hand being first carried very low and then brought near the lips), is in rude imitation of kissing the earth on which the Sovereign treads.

Whilst making these *salaams* the Sultan graciously

condescended to bestow a look, calm, and apparently indifferent as it was, upon us. A moment after these formalities our minister commenced his address; the Dragoman of the Porte occupying a position between him and the Sultan.

Mr. Marsh referred to the friendly relations existing between our country and the Sublime Porte, expressing his hope that they might ever continue.

He spoke of the interest which the people of the United States felt in the prosperity of Turkey, of the good wishes which he and those with whom he was officially associated personally entertained for His Highness, &c. His speech was made in French, and was translated, piecemeal, by the Court Interpreter into Turkish. The Sultan replied to each sentence in a low, scarcely audible tone, barely articulating the words. In fact it appeared to be an effort for him to talk *at all*, and perhaps he thought that we poor sublunary infidels, who were not, like him, destined to a paradise, where innumerable houris ravish with their charms, were not *worth* that effort.

He expressed his pleasure at the existing amicable relations between the two countries; his thanks for the kind wishes of the people of the new world and its Representatives to his Government; his hopes that the Minister would succeed, according to his wishes, in the mission upon which he was about to start, &c.

During the intervals which occurred in the delivery of his remarks he cast an occasional languid look upon first one and then another of us, which gave us a fine opportunity to scan his features.

He is rather low in stature, has dark, melancholy eyes, which exhibit an almost total lack of energy, but which have, at the same time, an amiable and benevolent expression.

The *tout ensemble* of his face is good, but on a careful inspection of it I discovered that it was much pitted with small-pox. Like most Mussulmans, he wears a full beard. He had a black cloth cloak thrown over him, which was fastened in front with a rich jewelled clasp. His coat was so richly embroidered, braided, and studded with diamonds, that it would be vain to attempt to describe it. The collar and cuffs were completely *encased* in diamonds. He wore a sword which reposed in one of the most elegantly chased gold scabbards that the most exalted fancy could conceive of. On his head was the red fez, which is universally worn, by high and low, throughout the Empire.

To our surprise, he remained standing all the time we were in His Royal presence, the unusual exertion attendant upon which, must have been quite fatiguing to His Highness.

His feet are very much inverted; but such is the case with those of most of the Turks, owing to the position in which they sit, their being so constantly in the saddle, and a certain custom of their infantile days, which modesty forbids me mentioning.

In surveying thus closely Abdul Medjid, his calm, apathetic expression, &c., I could not but reflect how essentially he differed from the late Sultan, his father, in those qualities which it is so important that a sovereign of a mighty country in these days of progress and political reform should possess.

Mahmoud the Second was energetic. He commenced and carried out many great reforms in his Empire. The awkward, bundling clothes of the soldiery were substituted by the snug-fitting garments of civilized Europe.

The Janissaries, that bloody band, long the terror of the Mahomedan Sultans and the inveterate enemies of reform, he effectually destroyed; a collection of costumed figures, in a Museum of Constantinople, being exhibited to the curious traveller to give him an idea of what they *once were.*

Many other important beneficial changes he accomplished, which it is unnecessary for me to mention.

The present Sultan I believe to be a man of most excellent heart, generous and kind. This was exhibited by the course he pursued toward the Hungarians, who found a safe shelter under the "Star and Crescent" when pressed by Austrian tyranny.

The liberal policy he pursues in reference to all Christians who dwell within his dominions is also worthy of all commendation, and far be it from me to detract in the least from his nobleness and magnanimity. But certainly he has not the strong mind and bold fortitude that his father possessed, nor do I think he makes the same effort to introduce reforms into his government.

The Empire is in *statu quo*, which, in this progressive age is the same thing as retrogradation.

The revenues, under the present system of raising them, are inadequate to the expenses of the government; whose functions, in consequence thereof, are considerably paralyzed.

Taxation is very unequal and unjust. The provinces, where the poor people have scarcely aught else but miserably small patches of soil to depend upon for their daily food, having the greater portion of the taxes to pay.

The great City of Constantinople, where exists so much wealth, pays nothing; so the unequalness of taxation, and the utter inability of such a system to meet the exigencies of the government, are clearly perceptible.

It really is to be hoped that the Sultan will, ere long, see clearly into this matter, and enjoin an *ad valorem* tax upon *all* property in his dominions; whether held by his own subjects or Franks. Should this be done there is no doubt but what the resources of the government would be adequate to its expenses.

But we must return to our main topic.

The speechification having been concluded, and Mr. Brown, with whom his majesty is personally acquainted, and for whom it appeared he entertains the highest esteem, having been presented as *Chargé d'Affaires* of the United States, we all took leave of His Highness in a manner which, owing to our number and inexperience in such matters, was somewhat embarrassing.

Keeping our faces turned toward the Sultan, we commenced a general "*backing-out*," only occasionally bumping against each other, or wounding the tender sensibilities of the toes in our rear. To a looker-on this scene must have been quite ludicrous and I should think the Sultan would enjoy such mightily, if the Koran allows him to laugh in the presence of unbelievers. As for ourselves, we were so ambitious to go through the ceremony gracefully, orientally, and safely, as to render us totally insensible to the humorous phase of it.

CHAPTER XII.

Visit to the Harem of the Minister of Foreign Affairs—The Effendi's Palace—Cavasses—Astonishing Number of Attendants—European Innovations—A Beautiful Eastern Picture—Coffee, Sherbet, and Pipes—A Point of Etiquette—Turkish Vanity—Rose Leaf Preserves—The Conservatory—A Little Eden—Bubbling Water, Flowers, Birds, and Sunshine—Sudden Appearance of a Eunuch—Accompanying Him into the Precincts of the Harem.

One day we visited the house of Fuad Effendi, then Minister of Foreign Affairs of the Ottoman Porte.

Mr. Brown's long intimacy and friendship with His Excellency procured for the ladies who accompanied us, a welcome admission into Madame Fuad's apartments, the Harem. This is an honor rarely accorded to those whom the followers of the Prophet are pleased to term "infidels."

After a short and delightful row on the Bosphorus, in one of those light and graceful boats called *caiques*, that glide over the surface of the water like an arrow sped from a bow, we found ourselves in front of the Effendi's palace.

On its marble steps, which are laved by the waters of the Bosphorus, we noticed the *cavasses*, or guards, their heads covered with the red fez, with its blue silk tassel, their coats thickly braided, and their swords slung to their sides, ready to receive us.

It astonishes an American to see the great number of attendants that a Turkish gentleman deems it necessary to have around him upon almost every occasion. If he be a Pasha, or Minister of State, it seems *impossible* for him to stir out without having a dozen, sometimes five times the number, running after him—some, should he be mounted, to attend to his horse; some as pipe-bearers; others as guards; and others still for what purpose no one can imagine, save it be the *effect* produced by their presence.

Fuad Effendi, on account of his rank, appeared to be pretty liberally supplied with them.

The steps ascended, we were conducted into a large and beautiful garden, then through a marble hall, and from thence into the reception-room.

Here, though we found everything elegant in the extreme, costly, and in the best taste, we perceived a decided innovation of European fashions and inventions. We soon noticed that the contiguity of Turkey with, and the intercommunication existing between it and more civilized countries, was rapidly revolutionizing the mode of living among the Orientals of the *better class, at least,* and had already wrought important changes.

We seated ourselves upon almost the only relic of the luxurious past, the *divan,* with the charming Bosphorus exposed to our view, whose placid bosom, reflecting many a mosque and gilded minaret, pillared palace, terraced garden, or tall dark cypress, adorning the opposite European shores, affords from the Effendi's windows a magnificent Eastern picture. We had not long composed ourselves before coffee was served to us. No stronger stimulant is ever used on such occasions.

This beverage always makes its appearance during a visit, whether social or diplomatic; and it is certainly very refreshing after a walk or ride, and whilst waiting to see the person upon whom you have called.

In summer, in addition to coffee, *sherbet* is served to the guest—a drink composed of the juice of the cherry, and cooled with snow from Olympus.

The coffee was brought as far as the door by *one* domestic on a rich salver, covered with a scarlet and gold-embroidered cloth, which was removed by *another* servant and thrown gracefully over the shoulder of the *first;* the coffee was poured out by a *third* attendant, from the same vessel in which it was made, into small china cups, each placed in a sarf, or outer cup, the latter composed of gold and silver and inlaid with precious gems. A *fourth* servant handed these around; and, after each guest had partaken of the coffee, pipes made of jessamine-wood with amber mouth-pieces, adorned with diamonds, were brought to the gentlemen.

Pipes, like the former article, are the invariable concomitants of a Turkish visit; and it is considered quite a breach of etiquette for a gentleman to refuse them, when proffered, whether he be a smoker or not —he must accept, and take one or two whiffs at least.

We have spoken of the richness of the pipes and the sarfs;—there is the same disposition to display these articles as there is on the part of a fashionable young lady to exhibit her jewelry; and, as the pipe and sarf appear so frequently before friends, there could be no better media for showing gemly wealth.

After we had smoked and chatted for a while, rose-leaf conserves were brought in. This is one of the most palatable and delicate preserves that could be conceived of, and is, I believe, peculiar to the East. Each guest takes but *one* spoonful—never any more, replacing the spoon on the *opposite* side of the waiter from whence he has taken it, to prevent its re-use; the morsel is then washed down by a mouthful of water.

The diminutive quantity taken reminds me of the fact, that in a Turkish house refreshments are *always* served up in homœopathic doses; it is only the constantly recurring participation of them that enables the "inner man" to derive any satisfaction from them.

These formalities having been concluded, we walked into the conservatory attached to the reception-rooms. This we found to be a perfect little Eden.

The first object that arrested our attention was a sea-nymph, which, resting on a rock, reared its marble front from out the centre of a circular basin of water, in which swam golden-hued fish. Over this was suspended a beautiful alabaster lamp, being one of a row that hung from the ceiling of the Conservatory along its median line.

Parallel to these, on either side, were suspended

two other rows of stained glass lamps, alternating with Gothic flower pots, in each of which latter, and clinging around it, were the most lovely running plants.

Along the sides of the Conservatory, and mounting up to the glass roofs, were ivies of every description; adjacent to which grew orange and lemon trees, laden with fruit; flower beds appeared here and there, and rustic seats made of iron.

The walks were paved with gravel mosaic, a style of paving very beautiful and very much in vogue in and near Constantinople.

The side of the summer-house which looked out on the flower garden was formed of stained and parti-colored glass.

Altogether, the effect produced by the commingling of such sweet associations, the bubbling of the water from the sea-nymph, the carolling of birds of strange notes and plumage, that found ready access to this fairy scene, the fragrance of the orange and the lemon, the beauty and the odor of the flowers, and the many beauteous hues which the bright sunshine, reflecting on the stained glass, cast over everything, was wonderfully fascinating.

Whilst we were enjoying these Paradisial scenes,

an *eunuch*, black as moonless midnight, clad in a scarlet robe lined with fur, suddenly made his appearance like the genii of old, and announced, in his uncouth vernacular, that he was ready to conduct our female friends within the sacred precincts of the *Harem*.

CHAPTER XIII.

Follow the Eunuch into the apartments of the Harem—Accompanied by Circassian slaves, ascend to Madame Fuad's Chamber—Luxurious Repose—Salutation—Madame Fuad's Manner and Occupations—Her Interest in her Slaves—Their Accomplishments—Turkish Female Dress—Unlike the "Bloomer"—Contentment of the Slaves—Female Slavery in the East a luxurious Captivity—Desire of the Young Circassian Girls to be sold into Slavery—Madame Fuad's Inquiries concerning Matrimonial Customs in our Country—Latticed Windows—Part with Her Ladyship—Serving of Refreshments—The Ladies return to the Salamnik—The Black Eunuch, the Guardian Spirit of the Harem—Fuad Effendi—His Intelligence and Reformatory Sentiments—His Garden—Miniature Lake—Swiss Cottage—Birds, Statues, &c.—Departure.

The eunuch led our friends through several large apartments into one comparatively small. Here they were received by two Turkish women, rather advanced in life, who were surrounded by about a dozen Circassian slaves.

By a wave of the hand the ladies were requested to be seated, and were informed, that on account of Her Ladyship being indisposed, she would be happy to see the visitors in her own chamber. In a short time the little daughter of Madame entered the room and said her Ma was ready to receive them.

With some of the slaves preceding, others following them, they ascended a wide, circuitous and splendid stairway, and were ushered into an apartment where, on a couch formed of green and yellow satin cushions, with a splendidly embroidered cloth of the richest hues and material thrown over her, surrounded by a host of fair Circassians and Georgians, one of whom was gently fanning her, gracefully reclined her Ladyship.

She partially arose on their entrance, and saluted them by carrying her right hand to her chin, and then quickly to her forehead.

Almost simultaneously with this salutation the slaves placed chairs in front of her, upon which our friends seated themselves; during this time other slaves remained standing about in different parts of the room ready to obey any summons of their mistress.

She expressed her regret at being unwell, and consequently unable to receive the visitors below; but the Oriental picture that she presented, thus reclining and thus surrounded, was far more interesting and attractive than it could otherwise possibly have been.

She appeared to be pleased with a visit by persons of the far off land of the New World, and asked about as many questions concerning America, as they did of her country.

They found her quite intelligent, and her manners easy and lady-like.

Women in the Turkish harems generally spend their time in luxurious indolence; but she evinced a great fondness for useful occupations. She manifested considerable interest in her slaves, and teaches them the art of embroidery, &c. Many of the slaves were skilled in music, and one of them, during the visit, played several Italian and Turkish airs on the piano. For the gratification of our friends, several of the most elegant dresses of Madame Fuad's wardrobe were exhibited, all of which were, of course, made in the loose and flowing style of the East.

The Turkish female dress cannot be called graceful; it can be made beautiful by rich working and material, but the *cut* of it is awkward.

It is very loose, and so long as to make it trail a foot or two on the floor: it is brought together just *above* the waist, by a Cashmere sash. In walking out the skirts are festooned up at the sides.

The "Bloomer," or as some designate it, the

"Turkish dress," adopted by a few, *very* few, bold ladies in America, bears no possible resemblance to the real article.

The slaves all appeared to be quite happy and contented, and more like daughters of their mistress than as her property. In fact, female slavery in Turkey is a mere nominal thing; the bondsmaid is taught every accomplishment, and frequently thereby marries the highest officer of the realm. The young Circassian slave who afforded our friends the musical entertainment, has since been married to Fuad Effendi's son.

At a first glance we would be inclined to pity the poor girl, fancying her forcibly torn from her unwilling and distressed parents, and sold into degrading servitude; but when we reflect that she, whilst still young, among her own kindred and amid her own mountain wilds, eagerly longs for the day that will bring her to this great Eastern capital, to be sold into such luxurious captivity, where she is cheered too by the bright beacon of hope, we cease to commiserate.

Madame Fuad was very anxious to know our practices concerning matrimony; whether it was customary with us to make the bride handsome presents, and whether a marriage is negotiated by others than the parties immediately interested, as is the custom in Turkey.

Our friends noticed the latticed windows which screen the inmates of the harem from the observation of outside barbarians ; from the interior a person can observe everything that is transpiring without ; and as an opera-glass lay on the satin couch near Madame Fuad, we can well imagine how the fair occupants of those harems which overhang the Bosphorus, amuse themselves by watching the ever-varying objects upon its surface.

After many social interchanges, her ladyship being pressing in her invitation to them to repeat their visit, our friends descended into a magnificently furnished apartment, where they were regaled with sherbet, brought to the door by the aforementioned black eunuch, and from thence by Circassian slaves to the guests ; each slave bearing a white, gold-embroidered napkin. When the refreshment was served, the attendants placed their hands on the lower part of their breasts, and retreated backward for a few paces, with their faces toward, and their eyes fixed upon, the guests.

The conversation with Madame Fuad was maintained through the assistance of Mrs. Brown and her beautiful Greek maid, Constantine; Mrs. B. translating the English into Greek, Constantine the Greek into Turkish, and *vice versa.*

The ladies now made their way toward the Salamnik, or male portion of the house, followed by several of the slaves, whose eagerness (caused by curiosity) in pushing forward, called forth the restraining interference of the black eunuch. This dark mass of flesh appeared to be the guardian spirit of the Harem. He keeps the keys, and without his co-operation the women can pass neither out nor in.

In the reception-rooms we all once more met.

His Excellency, Fuad Effendi, had made his appearance whilst our friends were in the Harem, and with him we had been enjoying, for half an hour, several relays of pipes.

He was extremely sociable, and expressed very liberal and enlightened political sentiments.

Being well educated, speaking the French language, and having travelled extensively on the continent, he had acquired quite a fund of information, and a very clear and intelligent idea of the workings of other governmental systems. He is imbued with that spirit which is calculated to work radical reforms in the Ottoman Empire, and assimilate it with civilized Europe.

After parting with our kind host, we wandered over his large and beautiful garden, where every species of shrubbery flourished.

Near the summit of the hill, in the rear of his house, which commands a fine view of the Bosphorus, the castles of Europe and Asia, Constantinople, the Marmora, Seraglio Point, &c., he has had excavated a miniature lake, an island occupying its centre, and connected with the main land by a small rustic bridge.

This lake was to be supplied with water from the mountain, which will tumble into it over rocks of lava.

On the margin of the lake is a little thatched Swiss cottage, which adds greatly to the picturesqueness of the scene.

Further down the hill are mammoth cages, containing hundreds of birds of the most varied and delicate plumage; whilst here and there lay statues and broken shafts from Egypt; stalactites from Broussa, &c., all of which, duly arranged, will adorn those beautiful grounds.

Once more at the palace gate, and soon in our *caique*, we left those enchanting scenes behind, which will ever linger in our memories like a bright and beauteous dream.

CHAPTER XIV.

The European Passport System—Its Annoyances—Unsuspiciousness of the Turks—The Sultan's Firman—A Translation of it, showing the Peculiar Style of Oriental Verbiage—Travelling in Turkey—Use Horses and Mules—The Camel—Transportation of Merchandize—Picturesque Effect of a Caravan of Camels—Magnificent Steeds—Scarcity of the Full-blooded Arab—A Ride to the Village of Belgrade—A Beautiful and Diversified Scene—Lady Mary Wortley Montague—Grand Aqueduct of Justinian—The Valley of Buyucdére — Godfrey de Bouillon — Return to Therapia.

In civilized Europe, out of Great Britain, the passport system, to use rather an unrefined expression, is a perfect bore. On leaving one country you must have the visé of the representative of the government whose territories you next intend entering; you must have the police visé, and that of the American Consul; and in some parts of Italy (Florence, for instance), when you wish to remain any considerable length of time in a city, it is necessary to procure from the Prefect of Police a *carti di soggiorno*, or card of sojourn.

All this causes much difficulty, delay, and inconvenience; especially in a country that is cut up into small principalities.

We should congratulate ourselves that in this free and happy country we can journey in all directions without the eternal annoyance of a passport; without watchful military officials asking us whence we came, or whither we are bound; or without being suspected of a disposition and the ability to cause a revolution or upset a government.

To enter Turkey does not invariably render the presentation of a passport necessary; in fact the Turks are much less particular and suspicious in regard to travellers, than any other people among whom we journeyed, with the exception of course of the English. When intending, however, to traverse the dominions of the Sultan, it is advisable to procure what is termed a *firman*. With this you can travel with impunity from one end of the empire to another.

As this document is written in the peculiar style of Oriental diction, I herewith subjoin a translation of it.

At the head of the paper, in large characters, stands the Toogha or monogram of the present Sovereign, containing the following words:

"SULTAN ABDUL MEDJID, SON OF SULTAN MAHMOUD—*May His Reign continue ever victorious!*

"PRIDE of the DOCTORS of HOLY WISDOM—the NAIDS and MUFTEES of the KAZAS (districts) situated on the route from MY SUBLIME GATE to the places hereafter mentioned.

"PRIDE of their EQUALS and COMPEERS, the EXECUTIVE OFFICERS and other PROVINCIAL CHIEFS,—may their power be augmented!

"On the receipt of the present EXALTED IMPERIAL and NOBLE CYPHER (monogram) be it known to you, that the LEGATION OF THE UNITED STATES of NORTH AMERICA, resident at MY GATE of FELICITY, has represented in a sealed note, that the AMERICAN GENTLEMAN (literally *Bey Zadeh or Prince Born*), named Mr. ———, has formed the design of travelling, for his own pleasure, to Egypt, Syria, Palestine, and the other countries in their neighborhood, requesting that the present NOBLE ORDER be issued in his behalf, for his protection and assistance whilst on said journey.

"Therefore YOU, who are the aforementioned OFFICERS, will be careful and attentive that the AMERICAN GENTLEMAN aforesaid, whilst on his way to and from the places previously stated, as well as at any places where he may be pleased to stop, be not, contrary to IMPERIAL TREATY between the UNITED STATES of AMERICA and TURKEY, incommoded by a demand for the payment of any taxes or dues, or any imposts whatsoever; nor be in any manner whatever molested; that he be protected and aided, be expedited on his way, peaceably; and in case of need that he be supplied with provisions at the current prices.

"This is MY IMPERIAL WILL and MY ROYAL COMMAND, and in this sense the present NOBLE FIRMAN has been issued. Be YOU therefore attentive to the execution of its contents.

"THIS KNOW and place entire confidence on the genuineness of the NOBLE CYPHER at the head of this FIRMAN.

"Written in the City of CONSTANTINE (Kanstantineh) in the MIDDLE IDES of the MOON of MOHANEEN, and the 1269th year of HEGIRAH."

Travelling in the East is generally performed on

horses and mules, as the roads are too rough for wheeled vehicles, and the shrill whistle of the locomotive has not yet awakened an echo in the valleys and forests of either European or Asiatic Turkey; it is consequently attended with much fatigue, especially if you use post horses, with which, changing every twelve or fourteen miles, you can make a distance of about eighty miles a day.

You pay so much an hour, and the speed at which you go depends pretty much upon the amount of *baksheesh* (presents) you give the *surroudjee* or postilion.

The camel is an animal that particularly arrests the attention of the traveller in the East.

In Turkey it is mostly used for the transportation of merchandize. Large caravans of camels may often be seen filing into Constantinople, laden with the rich commodities of Persia and Arabia.

Nothing can be more novel and picturesque, more truly *Eastern*, than the sight of a caravan of camels, moving slowly but steadily along, each animal accompanied by a venerable Turk or Arab, his long beard sweeping his breast, his ancient turban, his ample garments, and his rich Persian scarf bristling with Damascus blades.

The horses of Turkey, being descended from the Arab are finely shaped, full of mettle, and very swift. Even the most ordinary riding horse that can be hired for a few piasters at the foot of the steep hill of Pera, to carry you to the summit, is a fine-looking, sprightly animal. But walk into the stables of the Sultan or grandees, or witness a grand ceremony, such as the Sultan going to mosque, or such an one as that which occurs once a year within the walls of the *Old Seraglio* during the celebration of the *Bairam*, on which occasion all the principal officers of the realm are mounted, and you can behold some of the most magnificent steeds in the world; full of grace and noble bearing, as beautiful in their form and action as, under the circumstances last referred to, they are in their rich caparisons.

It is astonishing at what a low price a good horse may be purchased, an excellent one being obtainable for eighty dollars. The *real, full-blooded* Arab horse is scarce even in Constantinople, and the Sultan himself owns but few.

Whilst we were there, an English gentleman, Col. Williams, arrived from the frontiers of Turkey and Persia, where he had been acting as a commissioner to settle the boundary between the two countries, bringing with him several full-blooded Arab steeds, which he intended sending to England.

We fully tested the merits of the Eastern horses by taking many rides over the European hills adjacent to the Bosphorus, and through the lovely valleys opening into it.

One of these rides was to the village of Belgrade, where formerly resided the accomplished Lady Montague, and from whence so many of her charming letters were written.

The first part of our road wound along the border of a valley, smiling with the verdant luxuriance of summer. Deep, overhanging foliage, screened us from the rays of the morning sun, until, when in the upper part of the valley, we ascended a hill, from the summit of which we enjoyed a most delightful prospect.

Anteriorly the Black Sea, overhung by heavy clouds, presented its dark bosom to our view; in singular relief with which the old Genoese Castle, occupying the remotest Asiatic hill, exhibited a mingled and sublime scene of gloom and ruin.

On the right, far below us, the charming Bosphorus

laved the opposing shores of the two continents, whilst the clear horizon in the rear was fringed by the mosques and minarets of old Stamboul.

We enjoyed an ever-varying view of these beauteous scenes on attaining the summit of each succeeding hill, until we galloped into the lovely village of Belgrade; lovely in the picturesqueness of its situation and its rural quietude.

The house in which Lady Montague lived is still standing, but exhibits unmistakable evidences of the ravages of time.

On our return from Belgrade, we passed under the grand Aqueduct of Justinian, which, with a double row of arches, stretches across the upper portion of the valley of Buyucdére.

In the lower part of this luxuriant valley, charming not only on account of the beauty that nature has lavished upon it, but also because of the gaudy and picturesque costumes of its indwellers, flourish four or five magnificent plantain trees, under whose ample boughs, it is said, GODFREY OF BOUILLON encamped with his army of Crusaders in 1096.

This section of the valley is a favorite resort for the romantic youth of Buyucdére when "the silent hour of eve steals on."

From thence, keeping our course over the beautiful road that winds along the circuitous shores of the Bosphorus, we soon reached our temporary residence in the village of Therapia.

CHAPTER XV.

Mahomet's Injunctions as to Cleanliness—Ample Provision for a Supply of the Aqueous Element—Magnificent Baths, Fountains, Aqueducts, &c.—Bends of Belgrade—Doing in Turkey as the Turkeys do—Go through the Ordeal of a Turkish Bath—The Preparation Room—Change of Dress—Turkish Towels—Wooden Clogs—Enter a Room of Higher Temperature—After Preparation of the System enter a still hotter Room—Primitive Costume—The Operator—His Manipulating and Kneading Process—Sore Effects.

Of all the injunctions enforced by Mahomet upon his devoted followers, there is no one, save his precept urging them to constant prayer, so rigidly adhered to as that wherein he recommends the frequent ablution of the body in water.

For the latter purpose, as also for furnishing an abundant quantity of the pure element as a beverage, ample, provision is made within and around Constantinople by the construction of numerous and magnificent baths and fountains, as also extensive reservoirs and aqueducts for their supply.

Every one who visits the neighborhood of the great Eastern Capital is struck with the number, the vastness, and architectural beauty of the "Bends of Belgrade," and the immense aqueducts that convey their waters into the city.

The Baths are circular buildings. Some of those in the city proper are quite large, and the interior arrangements of them all are admirably adapted to the purpose for which they are used.

Notwithstanding I had heard terrible accounts of the severe rubbing and ducking with which I would be inflicted, still, acting in accordance with the old maxim, "when in Turkey, do as the Turkeys do," I made bold to go through the ordeal of a regular Oriental bath; and, in order to impart to the reader a correct idea of the general plan of the interior of a bathing establishment, as well as the bathing process, I cannot do better than furnish a short account of my experience.

The first or preparation room into which my bath attendant conducted me, was a large, circular apartment, with an arched ceiling, which had a skylight in the centre. A gallery, which extended around three-fourths of the room, was provided, at convenient distances from each other, with mattresses for the enjoyment of a siesta after the fatigues of the bath.

In this gallery I changed my street habiliments for others more appropriate to the occasion, the latter merely consisting of a couple of large Turkish towels properly adjusted.

Specimens of these celebrated towels took the premium at the World's Fair, at London. On one side they have a raised surface which renders them admirable absorbents.

Putting on a pair of wooden clogs, which had heels and soles some two or three inches high, to protect the feet from the warm marble floors, I descended from the gallery, and after many desperate efforts to keep said clogs under my feet, and much difficulty to avoid scattering the fire and tobacco of a dozen pipes that stretched out on the floor from the mouths of as many smoking Turks, I succeeded in gaining another and smaller chamber, possessing a much higher temperature than the former.

Here, on a mattress spread over a marble platform, I was under the necessity of reclining for about fifteen minutes, so as gradually to prepare my system for the endurance of the still higher temperature of the next apartment, into which my Turkish attendant now led me.

The atmosphere of this room was so warm and close, that it materially affected the respiration, and caused the perspiration to ooze from every pore.

There I was, attired something like our first great ancestors were in the Garden of Eden, just after they had partaken of the forbidden fruit; a single towel supplying the place of the fig leaf.

In this primitive state I was laid out, *sans cérémonie*, in a supine position, nothing but a blanket separating me from the decidedly hot marble elevation upon which it was spread.

The operator, a stalwart Turk, whose simplicity of attire equalled my own, now prepared for action.

Kneeling over me, he commenced by pressing gently on each rib, and the intercostal spaces, using both hands at the same time. Gradually the pressure increased, his well-practised fingers being introduced between the ribs in rather an insinuating manner.

After continuing this manipulation sufficiently long to make me feel peculiarly tender in that region, he commenced a kneading process just below the ribs, and his manual exercises over the epigastric and hypochondriac regions, almost convinced me that I was in a bakery, the proprietor of which had, in a sudden fit of absence of mind, taken me for a batch of dough, which he wished to work up as thoroughly as possible. However, the increased energy of action, on account of the sore effects it produced, both muscular and visceral, soon made me fully aware that I was not a mass of dough. Nevertheless, I endured all with as much grace and forbearance as possible, only manifesting my appreciation of such bodily torture by an occasional wry face, and a little muscular writhing.

CHAPTER XVI.

Bath continued—"A Used-up Man"—A Delicious State of Suspense—Not Quite Washed Away—Rough Scrubbing—Skinned Alive—Hold!—Enough!—"Macaroni"—A Coat of Lather—Almost Suffocated—The Bath Finished—Mummy Costume—Siesta—Remedial Advantages—Obesity of the Turks—Number of Bathing Establishments—Fountains—Expressive Inscriptions—Bounty of the Mahomedan Sultans—Propitiating the Prophet and Purchasing the Joys of Paradise.

After having cracked sundry joints and completely unstrung every fibre within me, rendering me altogether "a pretty well used-up man," my persevering operator varied the entertainment by carrying me into a small antechamber, where, from a fountain built in the wall, flowed a constant stream of water, under which he placed me and then left! Just imagine my feelings for the next ten minutes, during which time, in consequence of the attendant's absence, I was kept in a delicious state of suspense as to what would next ensue, and in regard to the length of time I would have to remain in that small room, which, under the circumstances, began to assume the appearance of a cell, in which the semi-barbarous wretch had incarcerated me? But now he has returned, and having discovered (to his great astonishment no doubt) that I am still alive and have not been washed away, he again takes me in hand.

He removed me from under the cascade, and, with his right hand covered with a coarse woollen glove, he commenced such a vigorous scrubbing over various parts of the body as to make me entertain serious apprehensions that I would pretty soon be fairly skinned alive!

I would fain have cried "Hold! enough!" but of what avail would these or any other Christian exclamations have been with a Moslem, acquainted only with his own wild mother tongue?

My only alternative, as in the former case, was to philosophically "grin and bear it," though the rubbing increased in intensity, and though successive rolls of the epidermis, in the baths familiarly termed "macaroni," were triumphantly laid out in parallel lines before my bewildered gaze! After this *truly refreshing* and *agreeable* occupation had been continued sufficiently long to leave me but a slight cuticular investment, I was as completely covered with a thick lather of soap as an Angola sheep is with wool; this was washed off by a Niagara of water, which, with the lather, entering the nostrils and causing the mouth to be closed to prevent a similar ingress there, came near producing suffocation.

With joy I now learned that the bath was finished, and after being enveloped like an Egyptian mummy, in the aforementioned towels, with one bound around my head in the form of a turban, I was reconducted into the large apartment I first mentioned.

Reclining on my mattress, with several long-bearded Mussulmans around me, who, robed in the same antiquated style, were enjoying themselves in the same *sans souci* manner, I whiled away a delicious hour of repose; completely abandoning myself to the luxurious relaxation consequent upon what I had just passed through, and regaling myself with coffee, sherbet, and pipes, furnished by Greek attendants. Thus do the more devout Mahomedans pass whole hours almost every day, observing the commands of their Holy Prophet in regard to cleanliness, and resigning themselves to a soft indolence amid the oblivious influences of tobacco fumes.

We will not dwell upon the obvious advantages arising from a bath of the nature I have attempted to describe; the revulsion, the healthy excitation of the various organs, the action upon the perspiratory glands, &c.

We think that the obesity and well-conditioned appearance of the Turks generally, women as well as men, are attributable to these daily ablutions.

But this is not the place for a medical dissertation.

There are over one hundred and twenty of these bathing establishments in and around Constantinople.

The fountains in the city and suburbs are very numerous and very beautiful; in fact they are among the chief ornaments of the place, and their style of architecture is quite peculiar. On all of them are gold inscriptions, in Arabic characters, on a blue ground, original, or extracts from the Koran; celebrating, in glowing terms, the praises of the liquid element.

The wayfarer is invited to partake of the refreshing draught, whose virtues far surpass the waters of the well of Paradise. He is told that *this* particular fountain was erected through the generosity of Sultan Achmet III., or *that* by the bounty of Sultan Mahmoud II., who, in these acts of benevolence and devotion, have obtained eternal favor in the eyes of their great Prophet, and secured for their souls the ravishing delights of Eden.

For the procurement of such infinite happiness, every Sultan erects either a mosque or fountain, which bears his name. He adopts this mode of pleasing *Allah*, as he cannot conveniently make a pilgrimage to Mecca, which, performed once in a lifetime, entitles the *Hadjee** to the joys of Paradise.

* A pilgrim.

CHAPTER XVII.

Religious Devotion of the Turks—Unjust Condemnation of Them—Prayer and Charity—The Koran—Example for Christians—Turkish Superstition—The "Evil Eye"—Charms—The Giant's Grave—Fatalism of the Turks—Apathy—Recklessness in Battle—Assurances of Happiness.

"GOD is Great and Mahomet is His Prophet." Thus exclaims and thus believes the Moslem devotee, as, on bended knee and half prostrate, he sends up his earnest supplications to Allah in the high heavens.

When the call to prayer, proclaimed by the *muezzin* from some towering minaret, summons the *faithful* to the worship of Jehovah, whether he is, when the sound falls upon his ear, amid the pleasure-seeking crowds which throng the Valleys of the Sweet Waters of Asia; whether in the presence of the true believer or infidel; regardless of the excitement around him or the criticising observations of the Christian, he inclines his face toward Mecca, and mutters his orisons with an earnestness and fervency, peculiar alone to the worshipping Mahomedan.

I have seen him on the deck of the crowded steamer, as she ploughed her way through the rushing waters; in some chosen spot by the margin of the winding Bosphorus, within his dark shaded cemetery, near the tomb of some friend, whose soul he believed had been wafted to the arms of Abraham; on the hillside and in the valley, place himself in an adoring posture, and become wholly engrossed in prayerful devotion.

We are too apt to condemn the Turk *in toto* on account of his peculiar religion. From afar we gaze upon and find fault with all the glaring defects of that religion, but never pause to admire its sublime truths and beauties.

We are shocked at the Prophet's allowing his followers a multiplicity of wives, but fail to admire the injunctions which recommend his votaries to constant prayer, deeds of charity, and acts of love.

The Koran, though the Bible of a false Prophet, contains many sublime precepts, the strict observance of which by their believers, affords an example that might be profitably imitated by thousands of pseudo

Christians in reference to the doctrines of Holy Writ.

Were the most of us as mindful of the teachings of the Son of God as the Mahomedan is of those of the Arabian Prophet, immorality would be a thing almost unknown among us, and our favored land would universally exult in the light of those Divine Rays that emanate from the Great Redeemer.

Yet, from the very nature of his belief, the Mussulman is superstitious to a very great degree; with this superstition, however, there is associated a primitive simplicity of manners, a uniform integrity and ingenuousness, that challenge admiration.

Among the singular superstitions of the Turks, the Arabs, as well as most Oriental nations, is crediting the existence of the "Evil Eye;" and the belief that certain prayers or signs, offerings or sacrifices, will avert its influence.

Amulets are worn by men and women, and suspended around the necks of the children.

The brute creation, too, is protected thus from evil, as the prancing charger is often seen with a huge charm adorning his forehead.

Nor do they stop here; even inanimate things become objects of solicitude, and it is no rare sight to see a dwelling protected from harm by the potent agency of a string of onions suspended from its eaves!

On the summit of the "Giant's Mountain," there is a grave, which some say is that of Joshua.

According to Turkish tradition, this mountain was once inhabited by a huge giant, so large that he could sit on the top and bathe his feet in the Bosphorus which laves its base.

Whatever may be the truth in the matter, the place is held sacred. The grave is enclosed, and an aged Moslem Dervish keeps his constant vigils near it. It is a shrine for the more infatuated Turks, and they often offer up their prayers within its sacred precincts.

Near it hang shreds of the garments of those who are suffering with disease, and who place them there, under the impression that healing virtues are derived from the pious act.

By the way, this grave is not over thirty feet in length, which fact would seem to conflict with the story that the *diminutive* individual in question could place his feet at the base whilst sitting on the summit; but the pious Dervish solves the mystery by contending that it only contains the giant's *big toe*. A single leaf from the Koran, or even a scrap of paper on which are written verses from that book, which he believes descended from the heavens, is highly cherished by the Moslem ; with this about his person he would consider himself invulnerable, and nothing would induce him to destroy it.

Should such a remnant meet his observation in the public highway, he would secure and protect it as a precious jewel.

The Turks are fatalists. They believe that Allah has pre-ordained every event, and a person will not question the sincerity of this belief when he witnesses the apathy with which they witness the progress of a disaster of which they are themselves the victims. Frequently, when their houses are being demolished by the fiery element, instead of using every exertion to extinguish the flames, they merely stroke their beards, look resignedly up to heaven, and exclaim "*Mashallah!*" (In the name of God!)

This doctrine of fatalism, in connection with the promise of Mahomet, that the souls of all those who are killed in the defence of the "faith" will be instantly transported to Paradise, renders the Turk, generally speaking, perfectly reckless on the battle-field.

Confident that he will either perish or survive according to the previous designs of Jehovah; fully satisfied that in either case he will meet a happy reward, in the former by being ushered into the midst of the Houris and Rose Beds of Eden, and in the latter by obtaining the favor of the Holy Prophet, he rushes boldly and fearlessly into the thickest of the conflict, unheeding and uncaring for the personal consequences.

CHAPTER XVIII.

Singular Beliefs—Hurried Burials—Funeral Practices—The "Questioning Angel"—The Soul Drawn out through the Mouth—The Mahomedan's Heaven—Celestial Houris—The Unbeliever's Heaven—Prejudices against Christians—Religious Liberty—The Turk's Attachment to his Religion—Rarity of his Conversion to Christianity—American Missionaries at Constantinople.

One of the most extraordinary beliefs of the Turks is, that the soul of a deceased person is in agony until the body is interred.

On this account, they hurry it off from the place of demise to the grave as speedily as possible; and it is indeed a curious and horrifying spectacle to witness a corpse, clad in sepulchral garb, placed upon a litter, which is borne upon the shoulders of four men, who are hurrying the body rapidly along to its final resting-place. The passer-by would think that they were trying to get rid of their friend in as summary a manner as possible.

To add to the novelty as well as the horror of this

sight, the looker-on can behold the *uncovered*, ghastly features, now rigid in icy death.

Only the male friends of the deceased accompany his remains to the grave.

Before he is taken from the house, prayers are recited over his body, and the ancient usage practised of washing the feet.

There are few, if any, ceremonies by the side of the grave.

The surviving relatives do not put on any habiliments of mourning, but sometimes the men manifest their grief for the loss of their kindred, by allowing their beards to grow to a prodigious length.

According to popular superstition, immediately after the body is interred, the "Questioning Angel" appears to the deceased, and propounds certain interrogatories; asking him if he has always been a good Mussulman, has always endeavored to please Allah, &c., &c. If his answers are satisfactory, his soul passes gently and imperceptibly from his body into all the untold delights of Paradise; but should the angel be *displeased* with the responses, the unfortunate defunct's soul is *drawn out through his mouth*, amid the direst torture, and consigned to the region of eternal darkness.

The Mahomedan's heaven is a place of ecstatic

bliss, where, in the midst of the most perfect beauty, the "*faithful*" will enjoy the companionship of thousands of the most lovely and ravishing houris.

The more obedient they have been to Mahomet's commands, the more beautiful and plentiful are the celestial fairies with whose presence they will be blessed.

The Koran assigns a *different* heaven, with an inferior degree of happiness in it, to us poor, outside unbelievers. Regarding us as "*infidels*," it deems it unreasonable to imagine that we can enjoy the same exquisite felicity as its votaries, in a future state.

There still linger some of the ancient prejudices against Christians, whom the Turks call *giaours*;* but they are rapidly disappearing, and now scarcely ever manifest themselves, save in some such fanatical season as the holy month Ramazan, which I have already partially described.

As far as the Porte is concerned, she appears to be extraordinarily well-disposed towards Christians; allowing them full religious liberty and every privilege they might reasonably desire, with the exception of holding landed property, in their own names, within her dominions.

* A word of contempt.

In Pera, the Frank quarter of Constantinople, there are several Greek churches, and in the chapel of the English Palace, the Protestant Episcopal service is held every Sunday morning.

The Turks are remarkable for their invincible attachment to their religion, almost every effort to bring them over to Christianity having proved utterly abortive. A single instance, almost if not the only one on record, of a Turk's changing the faith of his fathers, occurred whilst we were at Constantinople; and it produced so much excitement that the poor fellow found it necessary to leave the country.

The efforts of the enterprising and efficient American Missionaries in Turkey are directed, not to the conversion of the Islamites, but the Armenians and others, for the instruction of whose children they have established a school, wherein are taught the English language, and the bright, elevating truths and principles of Christianity.

CHAPTER XIX.

The Mahomedan Sabbath—Separation of the Sexes in the Mosques—Peculiar Mode of Worship—Requirements to gain Admittance into the Mosques—How obtained—Bayard Taylor and his friend Harrison—Harrison having succeeded in visiting Mecca in the guise of a Turk, attempts to enter a Mosque in the same Costume—Is detected—Beats a Retreat—Mosque of St. Sophia—A sacred Repository of Valuables.

In Turkey, as in most other countries whose religion is a nationality, those occupying an humble position in life are much more enthusiastic as well as sincere in their religious devotions than others, who, by being in a more exalted position, pecuniarily or politically, have their minds vitiated by luxury or the strife for high places.

Yet are the latter far from lacking respect for, or obedience to, the requirements of their creed.

The highest dignitaries of the land, not excepting the Sultan himself, scarcely ever allow the sun to perform his diurnal circuit without prostrating themselves before the throne of Allah.

Friday is the Mahomedan sabbath. On that day the mosques are open, and their matted floors covered with the kneeling and cross-legged faithful.

The women are permitted to worship in the mosques, but are compelled to form themselves into a distinct group, somewhat remote from the men.

Though the Mufti sometimes officiates, yet frequently no one acts in the capacity of preacher; each worshipper, with his face turned toward the Holy City, serving the Most High in any manner that corresponds with his individual inclination.

It is a very novel sight to see a large number of Mussulmans engaged in their peculiar devotions.

Whilst some are kneeling with their eyes turned heavenward, others are standing erect, their arms crossed over their breasts; whilst others still are so humbly prostrated, that their foreheads touch the floor—all are muttering their prayers, and these different postures accord with the strength and fervency of the different passages in the prayers.

Every one who enters the mosques must take off his shoes at the door, and put on slippers.

This rule is imperative, and applies to the believer as well as the unbeliever. To provide for its observance, you must have slippers of your own—your cavasse, or servant, making the change for you, and taking charge of your shoes until your return.

Franks cannot gain admittance into the mosques without the procurement of a *firman*, or permit, from the Sultan.

It is also necessary to have a *cavasse* of the Porte, who acts in the double capacity of guide and guard, and whose presence testifies to the Turks that their worthy sovereign has granted you the privilege of traversing their holy sanctuaries. With these accompaniments you need not be under any apprehension of being interfered with by even the most fanatical.

Strangers obtain the *firman* through the agency of their respective Legations, and when intending to go through the mosques, form a party of about a dozen persons.

On the occasion of our visit, we enjoyed the pleasure of Bayard Taylor's company.

Taylor had just returned from his extensive travels in Africa, from whence he had written many interesting letters to the New York Tribune.

His friend, Harrison, of Kentucky, who journeyed with him, was also one of the party.

These gentlemen travelled through the East in full Oriental costume; and, speaking a little Arabic, at the same time having suitable personal appearances, passed muster as very good Mussulmans.

Harrison was clad *à la Turque* when with us. One day he attempted to enter a mosque without a firman. He was flushed with confidence, inasmuch as he had, clad in his Eastern guise, with his flowing beard, and smattering of Arabic, succeeded in accomplishing what very few Christians *ever have accomplished*, viz.: a pilgrimage to Mecca, kneeling and muttering his prayers, with the most faithful and devout. It so happened that a Turk recognized him as a gentleman whom he had, a day or two previously, observed holding a very animated conversation, in good Anglo-Saxon, with the American *chargé*; and knowing that none of *his* countrymen could perform such a lingual miracle as that, he made his way towards Harrison with no very amiable expression on his countenance.

Our friend, observing his advance, concluded that discretion was the better part of valor, and beat a retreat, making good his escape from the vicinity of the mosque ere the virtuous indignation, occasioned by his intrusion, had gathered into a storm.

It is superfluous, I think, to furnish the reader with a description of the mosques, as those noble Moslem temples, that constitute the chief features in the beautiful tableau that *Old Stamboul* presents to the greedy eyes of the voyager as he rounds the Golden Horn, have been so frequently and so faithfully described by others more competent to the task than myself.

Who has not read of St. Sophia, with its immense dome, that appears to be suspended in the heavens; its columns of many-hued marbles, and its ceilings of mosaic? Once the pride of the *Christian* world, it still, though stripped of much of its pristine grandeur, stands the acknowledged wonder of the *Mahomedan.* It is not my province to speak of matters with which it is presumed almost every one is familiar, but merely those, which, from their *apparent* insignificance, or from some other cause best known to themselves, book writers generally neglect to mention, knowing that these subordinate matters exemplify, as much as any other, the peculiar characteristics of the people among whom they exist.

To discover one of these peculiarities, let us pause for a moment, and look up into the gallery of St. Sophia. There we see an innumerable quantity of boxes, packages, and every conceivable article of value; piles of money, diamonds, &c. What does it all mean? The house of prayer is assuredly not to be converted into a place for barter? No, these valuables are merely placed there for safe keeping. Their owners have gone on a pious pilgrimage to Mecca, and have left their property there, under the firm conviction that no sacrilegious hand will harm it during their absence. *There* it is doubly safe, as besides not being exposed to the dangers of the devastating fires which so frequently afflict Constantinople, it is *impossible for a Moslem to commit any act of dishonesty within the sacred precincts of a sanctuary dedicated to Allah and the Prophet.*

CHAPTER XX.

The Sultan Going to and Returning from Mosque—Brilliant Procession—The Royal Barge—A Moslem Summons to Worship—The Howling Dervishes of Scutari—Their Thrilling Ceremonies—Wild Fanaticism—Torturing Instruments—Closing Scenes—The Whirling Dervishes of Pera—Exclusion of the Females—Learned Patriarchs.

THE Sultan going to, or returning from mosque, affords one of the most interesting, as well as imposing spectacles to be witnessed in the Turkish Capital.

He is, if on land, mounted on a magnificent and richly caparisoned Arab charger. Two or more riderless horses follow in his wake, each with superb trappings, and, like the animal on which he rides, led by formidable-looking grooms.

The Military Body Guard of His Majesty, and sometimes a few high dignitaries, the latter in the saddle, form a part of the brilliant procession that attends His Highness on such occasions.

On the Bosphorus he glides in a highly wrought *caique*, propelled by sixteen *caiquejies*, who, with a long simultaneous sweep of the oars, fairly make the barge fly over the water.

The *caique* which he occupies, in which, cross-legged, he sits under a royal canopy, is preceded by two others that go before to herald the approach of the "RULER OF THE UNIVERSE," and to intimate to all the boats scattered over the Bosphorus that His Excellency must have a wide margin to move in.

"The sound of the church-going bell" is unheard in Constantinople proper, the hour of worship and of prayer being announced from the minarets by the muezzim, whose prolonged cry—*La Allah; illah, Allah Mohammed resoul Allah* (there is but one God and Mahomet is his prophet), as it falls upon the silence of eve, has a truly singular effect.

As among religious sects in general, there are some whose peculiar rites distinguish them as a distinct division of the body ecclesiastical, so among the Mahomedans there are those, who, holding the same tenets in the *main*, as the rest of their religious brethren, yet whose still more singular mode of worship constitutes them a separate people.

I have reference to the Howling Dervishes of Scutari and the Whirling Dervishes of Pera.

It would be impossible for pen and ink to give an adequate idea of the wild antics, and the still wilder guttural sounds, that characterize the religious exercises of the former, or the rigid countenances and peculiar rotary motions of the latter. Each sect performs once a week.

The *first* part of the ceremonies of the Howling Dervishes is quiet enough; principally consisting in prayer and an embracing of each other, and their venerable Patriarchs, who occupy a position in the upper part of the room corresponding with the direction of Mecca.

But the excitement and fervor grow apace; a deep sepulchral howl soon becomes conspicuous in the ejaculations; a phrenzied expression sits upon their countenances; they walk with hurried steps, and among each other, in many a giddy maze; wilder become the howls, wilder the visages, more rapid the devious pace. Club-shaped instruments, with bulbous ends set with iron points, are wielded high in the air, and brought down with great *apparent* force upon their naked bodies; sharp swords are driven into them by a cudgel's heavy blows; the points of heavy iron weapons are placed upon the eye, and then twirled upon that delicate organ.

At length, after the excitement has attained the highest pitch; the cries have become like those of the raving maniac; their motions of unsurpassable violence; and their blood, made to flow by self-inflicted hands, has crimsoned their bodies, they are carried out fainting and exhausted from the scene of their religious zeal.

It is said that in the Barbary States, in certain seasons, these Dervishes become so furious in the midst of their unique performances, that they rush out into the streets, with the instruments of torture in their hands, and wo betide the unfortunate son of Israel who *then* happens to cross their path; he would almost certainly fall a victim to their wild fanaticism.

The Whirling Dervishes are more peaceable. Commencing their religious rites in the same manner as their howling neighbors, they continue them by a steady, whirling motion, with their arms extended and their eyes cast downward.

With their heads surmounted by sugar-loaf shaped, brimless hats, and their loose skirts, whose lower margins, in the act, describe a perfect circle, round, round they go, unceasingly for hours.

Women are not allowed to participate in the ceremonies of either the Howling or the Whirling Dervishes.

In the mosque of the latter were—I say *were*, for, since our visit to it, the mosque has been destroyed by fire—latticed windows in the walls, through which the Turkish females peeped at their rotating masculine lords.

I would here remark, that the undue zeal manifested by these strange sects is condemned by the *mass* of Mahomedans; and I would also do them the justice to say, that many of their venerable and patriarchal members are men of great learning and research.

CHAPTER XXI.

Turkish Cemeteries—Their Vastness—Cemetery of Scutari—Cypress Trees—Turbaned Stones—Mingled Scene—Carvings and Inscriptions—Eyoub—Character of the Epitaphs—Examples—Woman's Soul.

As a fitting topic to succeed what I have said about the religious devotions and superstitions of the Turks, I will now make a few remarks concerning the Mahomedan cemeteries, whose vastness and singularity arrest the attention of every sojourner at Constantinople, causing him to feel, as doth almost every object his eye dwells upon in the Orient, that he is indeed in a strange land, and amidst a strange and peculiar people.

Taking an elevated, central position, such as that on the top of the Seraskier's Tower, we command a fine view of numbers of those almost boundless forests of dark cypress trees, within whose profound shade the monuments of millions of defunct Turks rear their turbaned heads. We will discover that they form a very distinguishing feature in the magnificent picture spread out around us.

The largest and most interesting is the Cemetery of Scutari, on the Asiatic side of the Bosphorus. This cemetery is over three miles in length. The cypress trees, tall and slender, like the minarets attached to the mosques, being thickly planted, and the tombstones occupying in some places almost every foot of ground left vacant by the trees, render it an extremely difficult matter for a person to wend his way through these fields of the dead, except over the main path.

Nothing can excel the startling effect of the dark mingled view of tombs and cypress trees.

Many of the stones are capped by the Tarbouch, or the turban; the ample and painted folds of the latter resembling so much the genuine article as to induce one, on a hurried glance through the *Champs des Morts*, to fancy it crowded with venerable Moslems who are standing as sentinels over the graves of departed friends.

The inscriptions, as well as the ornamental designs, are in relief, and generally gilded.

Many of the marble slabs are painted a gaudy

color, their bright hues affording a strange contrast with the cypress' gloomy shade.

Some are carved and gilded with much elegance and good taste; but as a general thing they do not present an appearance that corresponds with our idea of beauty. Only occasionally you see them surrounded or protected by any kind of enclosure; but those at Eyoub, up the Golden Horn, are first walled in and screened by wire-work that rises like an arbor above them. These are really elegant, and are the tombs of distinguished characters. Hard by these tombs is the mosque wherein the Sultans of Turkey gird on the sword of Othman.

The epitaphs, which are either original or extracts from the Koran, do not so much record the virtues of the deceased as they furnish admonitions to the living.

In order to give an idea of their tone and sentiment, I herewith subjoin a few specimens, translated from the Arabic, in which language they are carved:—

HIM, THE ETERNAL AND EVERLASTING!

Death is a cup, out of which all must drink;
The shroud, a garment in which all must be dressed;

The hearse, a carriage in which all must ride;
The grave, a door through which all must pass;
The earth is a home where all must dwell;
From God all came, all must return to Him.

Say a Fatha (opening chapter of the Koran) for the soul of ORMAN AGA. 1252.

HIM, THE ETERNAL!

My SADIKA has gone,
Alas! Alas!
My darling child has left me,
Alas! Alas!
SADIKA! the light of my eyes,
The rose garden of my hopes,
Has gone to Paradise.

Pray a Fatha for SADIKA, the daughter of OSMAN BEY. A. H. 1256.

HIM, THE ETERNAL AND EVERLASTING!

Alas! AHMED BEY'S wife has left this passing scene;
Unfortunate woman, she had to forsake her ten young children;
May she be immersed in the Sea of Mercy of the All Just!
With eyes filled with grief's tears I write her epitaph;
The Eternal in His mercy has taken my Shemsieh Kadin.

HIM, THE ETERNAL!

Scarce had I become a mother and seen my new-born child,
When the arrow of destiny sent my soul into Eternal Life:
I left the garden of this world for that of Paradise.

Say a Fatha for AYESHA, wife of ORMAN EFFENDI.

HIM, THE ETERNAL!

Passer-by, look a moment at this my tomb. If you are wise, be not neglectful, but seek wisdom at its source (Religion). I was a heedless wanderer; what sorrows have I not met with? At their close I became earth, and this stone is placed above my head.

IBRAHIM EFFENDI'S wife, say a Fatha for her soul.

After reading the aforegoing epitaphs we would not be inclined to coincide with the generally entertained opinion that the Mahomedan denies a soul to woman; though, with Moore, he may believe that "reason and thinking are out of her sphere."

CHAPTER XXII.

"Down Among the Dead Men"—Female Resorts—Tombstones of the Females—Of the Janissaries—Separate Burying Grounds—Characteristics of the Turkish, Armenian, Jewish, &c., Cemeteries—Disinclination of the Turk to be Buried in European Soil—His Belief as to the Ultimate Fate of European Turkey—Consolation at the Close of his Mortal Career—Mausoleum of Mahmoud II.

NOTWITHSTANDING the superstitious nature of the Orientals, they appear to have no dread of being near the buried dead. On the contrary, the cemeteries are among the favorite haunts of both men and women.

I have seen those cemeteries which border on the Bosphorus filled with the Turkish females, who, wrapped in their gaily colored *ferigees* and white *yashmaks*, formed, amidst the leaning marble slabs and cypress trees, many a picturesque group.

There, with naught but the grass-covered earth or the cold marble slab as carpet or divan, will they while away many an hour; chatting, smoking, partaking of refreshments, surveying themselves in small mirrors, or watching the countless, varied, and interesting objects passing before them on land and water, as well as the frolicsome evolutions of their gaily dressed children, of whom, especially the boys, they are excessively proud.

The tombstones of the females are simply distinguished by a rose branch being carved on them; and the style of the turban surmounting those of the male denotes the rank of the departed.

The stones designating the graves of the once formidable and bloody Janissaries are clearly distinguishable by their being decapitated; their turbaned heads having been struck off by the infuriated populace, simultaneously with, or soon after the destruction of that sanguinary band.

As the Turk, the Armenian, the Jew, and the Frank, has each his particular quarter to *reside* in, so has each his separate and distinct section to be *buried* in.

The tall and gloomy cypress and the leaning, turbaned stones, are peculiarly Mahomedan; a horizontal position of the latter, with a slight elevation and rude devices carved on them, showing the trade or profession of the deceased, or circular holes for the birds to slake their thirst in after refreshing showers, characterize the Armenian; simple marble slabs lying flat on the ground denote the Jewish burial places; whilst those of the Frank exhibit the usual features of a Christian place of interment for the dead.

On account of the Turks believing that European Turkey will ultimately pass into the hands of the *Giaour* or Christian, they prefer being buried in Asiatic soil. Hence the immensity of the great cemetery of Scutari, in which lie, in eternal repose, as many bodies as would correspond in number with twenty times the present population of Constantinople! Contemplating the nature and tendencies of his religion, we can well imagine how repugnant the idea must be to a Turk, that after he has bidden farewell to the scenes of this world, his mortal remains will be sacrilegiously trodden over by the rude foot of the "infidel." And we can also conceive his resigned expression, when dying, and the sincere, fervent, "God be praised" that comes from his lips, in that solemn hour, when he realizes the consoling assurance that sacred Moslem earth will, for successive ages, conceal his body within its hallowed depths.

In the city of Constantinople are several magnificent Mausoleums, containing the bodies of Ottoman Sovereigns.

One of the most beautiful of these is that of the present Sultan's father, the late Sultan Mahmoud; whose remains repose therein, enclosed in an elegant sarcophagus, which is covered with the finest shawls of Persia and Cashmere, and has its head surmounted by a genuine turban of the olden time.

The sleepless vigilance of a pious Mussulman shields from sacrilegious touch this last sacred resting-place of the "Refuge of the World."

CHAPTER XXIII.

The Ramazan, or Holy Month—Rigid Observances—Religious Fanaticism—Ancient Prejudices dying out—Changes for the better—Their causes—A Confused Scene—Afloat—Large Number of *Caiques*—The Oblivious Turk—Female Curiosity—The Bazaar Boat—A Polyglot Scene—The Great Variety of Languages Spoken in the Orient—Illumination in Honor of the Descent of the Koran—Brilliant Scene at *Tophané*—Constantinople Illumined by Olive-Oil-Fed Lamps—The Ships in the Golden Horn lit up.

In a previous chapter I made reference to the Ramazan, or Holy Month; a season set apart by Mahomet for fasting, for prayer, and for a rigid abstinence from all the usual indulgences of life.

Religious fanaticism is more apparent now than at any other season.

The conviction is more deeply rooted in the heart of the Moslem that his is the only true religion, that there is but one God, and that Mahomet is his Prophet.

Now rankle in his breast those feelings of enmity toward the *Giaour*, that in former days, when more complete barbarism overshadowed his land, urged him to wield aloft the glittering scimitar, and bring it down dripping with the life-blood of the dying Christian.

Now do no sensual gratifications interfere with his fervent anticipations of future bliss; in fancy he dwells within his Moslem heaven; for the prayers he recites, the self-denial he practises, the charity he bestows, his faith in Allah, his confidence in Mahomet's promises, his exhibition of hatred toward all infidels, combine to assure him that naught but Paradisial joys await his wafted spirit.

The prejudices and fanaticism of the season are, however, losing the intensity of former years. No longer is it hazardous for the Christian to appear in the crowded streets of Stamboul. No longer is it necessary, save on special occasions, to be guarded by some formidably armed Mustapha.

Nor even is that honorable pioneer of civilization and moral advancement, the Christian missionary, who "goes forth into all lands," to preach the Gospel of the Saviour of mankind, molested in his holy vocation, but preaches, undisturbed, his saving doctrines, within sound of the muezzim's call to prayer.

These facts exhibit the radical changes for the better that are gradually taking place in the Ottoman Empire; they show the effects of a European infusion of population and ideas; that antiquated notions are expiring, their place being supplied by new and more reformatory ones, which, developing themselves insensibly, though surely, will, in course of time, place Turkey in that attitude among the nations of the earth that her territorial extent and geographical position so eminently entitle her to.

As I have already, in the eleventh chapter, referred to Medjid's want of energy, as compared with his father, it is appropriate that I should here remark that these changes for the better of which I speak, are not superinduced by any direct interference of the Sultan, but indirectly by the free scope and latitude of speech and action, which his liberal policy gives to Europeans resident in his dominions.

But to a particular incident of Ramazan. On the last night of this month is celebrated the descent of the Koran from the heavens.

This celebration we were so fortunate as to witness whilst at Constantinople.

It was evening; and after descending the "Infidel

Hill" of Pera, and working our tortuous way through a perfect labyrinth of Turks, Greeks, Jews, Arabs, donkeys, dogs, &c., we arrived at Tophané; where, in the midst of the utmost confusion, produced by the *caiquejies* of a hundred *caiques*, vying with each other which could scream the loudest to arrest our attention, we managed to get afloat.

A few strokes of the oars carried our light boat out into the stream. A thousand other *caiques* were shooting about in all directions, and the frequent cry of "*Guarda!*" "*Guarda!*" called our attention to the interesting fact that if we did not cave our backs in a little, or somewhat incline our heads, the sharp bow of one might give us a severe "dig" in the spine, or enter unceremoniously into the cranial region.

But soon we were half way to Seraglio Point, where we "hauled up" in the midst of a legion of *caiques*, all filled with an eager, chattering, motley crowd of men, women, and children.

In a boat, on one side of us, were squatting half a dozen Turkish women; an old Turk was sitting a little aft, so wrapped up in two absorbing feelings, one created by the glorious wreaths of smoke, which in a cloud rose from his well-filled *chibouk;* the other by the self-satisfying consciousness that six beautiful concubines were ever ready to attend his bidding, that he was almost oblivious of the excitement and the "busy notes of preparation" around him. He actually forgot what he came out to see. His women though were not so idle; they were all astir. If we watch them closely, now that darkness is quickly following in the footsteps of twilight, and their husband cannot so easily detect their improprieties, we will discover that they have withdrawn their *yashmaks* a little, so as to give themselves a fair "look out." *They* are not going to miss anything, we may be satisfied of *that;* and if we scan those large, busy, peering eyes of theirs, and listen to that avalanche of words, whilst they are criticising the scenes around them, we will be doubly assured of this fact. Another boat near us was overrunning with a crowd, among whom we could recognize the representatives of every European country. It was the Bazaar boat, a sort of river omnibus. Here the red *tarbouch* of the Oriental, and the stove-pipe section hat of the Frank; the ample turban of the olden time, and the peaked head-covering of the Persian, formed a mingled and curious scene.

Here we heard a terrible jabbering of Turkish, Greek, Italian, French, &c.; all these languages being equally well spoken by the party, either rapidly alternating with each other, or all coming out together in one grand volley.

This reminds us of the fact, that a knowledge of the different languages is almost universal among the inhabitants of the Frank quarters of not only Constantinople, but of all the large seaboard cities of the East. You are going along the streets of Pera, and notice a group of females discussing—some scandal it may be; curiosity prompts you to halt—you observe closely the gesticulations, the words, the very *accent*, and make up your mind that *Italian* is their vernacular. You have no sooner come to this conclusion, than the conversationists slide imperceptibly into *French;* they rattle away in such a free style, that you are inclined to the belief that they have just arrived from Paris, where they must have lived ever since they were born. Such a thought, however, is soon drowned by a cataract of *Greek;* then come in rapid succession *Turkish*, *Armenian*, &c., until you are satisfied that you might as well endeavor to *stop the women from talking altogether*, as to detect their nationality. Why, an acquaintance with three or four languages appears to be an *innate attribute* of the Perotes.

But to resume.

As far as the vision extended, we discovered, on every side, that the Golden Horn and Bosphorus were literally covered with boats; and great was the confusion produced by the rapid plying of the oars and the unearthly screeching of the *caiquejies*, in their efforts to get into favorable positions to witness the Grand Fete in honor of the Descent of the Koran. When we cast our eyes toward Tophané, what a magnificent and brilliant scene they rested upon.

All along the shore was a continuous flame; whilst high up in the air, between the lofty tops of the tapering minarets, appeared in blazing characters the words, "MY SOVEREIGN, MAY YOU LIVE A THOUSAND YEARS!"

Constantinople itself looked like a fairy scene. Millions of diminutive lamps, fed with olive oil, shed their brilliancy over the seven hills. Strange convolutions, too, these lights assumed. He that could read Arabic or the language of the Turk would have been able to discern, in those hieroglyphics glowing in the heavens, sentiments of beauty and of piety, borrowed from the Koran, or generous wishes for the prosperity of the beloved sovereign of the Ottomans.

The ships in the Golden Horn; the ponderous gun-ships of the Sultan; and the steamers that ply on the Bosphorus, furnished their quota to the general illumination. The outline of each was easily traced—the bulwarks, ropes, and masts presenting diverging lines of light.

CHAPTER XXIV.

Turkish Soldiery—Grand Pyrotechnic Display—Firing of Cannon—A Calm—The Royal Barge—Sultan Abdul Medjid—He Prays—Effulgent Display—Annual Presentation of a new Wife to the Sultan—Self-denial of his Highness—Return to Shore—Ascend the Heights of Pera—The Turkish Guard, Mustapha—A dense and heterogeneous Throng—Its Turbulent Elements—Dangerous Proximity—One of our Female Companions alarmed—Summary mode of Stealing a Watch—An exciting Struggle—Arrive safely at Home.

On the smooth parade-ground that skirts the water-front of the mosque Tophané stood long files of Turkish soldiers, with their myriads of glistening bayonets.

Details from these were actively engaged in firing off heavy cannon, whose reverberating thunders were enough to start Jove from his "cloud-capped" throne. A wheel of vast proportions was there revolving, and throwing out various-colored fire; rockets were fizzing, cracking, and scattering their fiery splendors in the upper regions of darkness.

Nor are these demonstrations long confined to Tophané; other sections catch the spirit, and soon the booming of a hundred cannon is heard in all directions. The leviathan gun-ships of the Sultan, the war-vessels of Russia, Austria, England, and other European nations, that lie anchored out in the stream, add their thunders to the mighty roar.

One would fancy that the Russian Bear had attacked the Porte in her own waters, and that the fleet of the latter, in conjunction with the "Allies," was opening its terrible batteries upon the grim enemy of the North.

Had iron balls been hurled in as rapid succession as one report of cannon followed another, and had each rocket been a bomb-shell, that night the Golden Horn would have poured blood from its mouth, and the shattered mosques, palaces, houses, &c., of the City of the Sultan, would have imparted an awful feature to the picture of the morrow.

But now there was a calm; and over the unruffled bosom of the waters, in which many a gem of light sparkled, nought could be heard save the occasional splash of an oar, or the subdued voices of the Greeks urging their *caiques* into line, to leave a clear space for the Royal Barge, which was rapidly approaching, bearing, seated under a silken canopy, the "Ruler of the Universe."

As though it had the wings of an eagle, away flew the Imperial *Caique* to the landing-place of Tophané; where, greeted by a military salute, and the enthusiastic cry of "Long live Sultan Abdul Medjid!" the Ottoman Sovereign steps ashore, and a moment afterwards is kneeling upon the matted floor of the Mahomedan Temple hard by, pouring out his soul's devotions to the Great Allah and His Prophet. Fervid were his prayers that night, for it was the anniversary of the descent of the Holy Book from the heavens; and deeper into his heart sank the everlasting conviction, that "God is Great and Mahomet is His Prophet."

His prayer finished, he was conducted to the water's edge, where sixteen lusty oarsmen were ready to speed him to his palace by the Bosphorus; and whilst their rapid oars were scattering the parted waters, we were bewildered by the grandeur and ineffable splendor of the display around us. Roman lights, fire-wheels, rockets, &c., imparted a noontide effulgence to the midnight sky, whilst again broke upon the ear the fulminations of a thousand cannon,

14

Such were the public demonstrations. Would that we could step with you, kind reader, across the portals of the Imperial Mansion, and gaze upon the ancient rites within its sacred precincts. Interesting indeed they were, for on that night took place the presentation of a new wife to the Sultan; one selected for her matchless charms from among the fairest of Circassia's daughters.

This ceremony occurs annually. Unfortunate gentleman, he has to be content with getting a new wife only once a year! However, let us moderate our sympathy, by reflecting that during the twelve months his self-denying Highness can revel in the smiles and caresses of four *odalisques*, and between two and three hundred beautiful female slaves.

Leaving the Sultan to the full fruition of his joys, let us direct our course towards the shore; for the iron-mouthed monsters have ceased their din, the olive-oil-fed lamps are either extinguished or become dim by burning, and the stick of the last rocket has floated into the Marmora.

We soon effected a landing. Even the jostling together of a hundred *caiques*, our own among the number, and the terrible stride we were compelled to make from the boat to the dilapidated quay, failed to succeed in furnishing us with an extemporaneous bath.

We had now the heights of Pera to mount, through the narrow, steep, and crooked streets of that town. Mustapha, our guard, with his hand reposing upon his venerable sword, marched before us to shield us from molestation. (This faithful Turk has been one of the guards of our Legation, at Constantinople, for many years; he was such during the time that Commodore Porter was Minister at the Sublime Porte.)

A crowd pressed forward in the same path with us. We had scarcely passed the Turkish Café, near the water, and neared the beautifully constructed and gilded Fountain of Tophané, before the throng became so dense that we could scarcely make headway through it.

Such a heterogeneous, moving human mass was never seen before. The Christian was there, curiosity and a love of sight-seeing being the motives that induced him to risk his life out that night; the Mohamedan was there, his religion having prevented him from courting Somnus, ere he had witnessed the grand fête in honor of the Descent; the Greek was present, taking advantage of the press to gratify his thieving propensities; the wily Persian and the Jew, the Bedouin Arab, and the uncivilized Koord, swelled the human tide. The confusion of languages was worse than that heard around the Tower of Babel, and the variety of dress made that narrow pass the kaleidoscope of the costumes of the world.

The turbulent elements of this mixed assemblage soon became manifest; with no exercise of volition on our part, we were carried forward as upon a billow, or tossed from side to side. A cross current set in, and separated us from a portion of our company, which was mostly composed of ladies. Men, whose belts presented a formidable array of knives and pistols jostled against us, whom a mere whim might have induced to test the qualities of either weapon upon their immediate neighbors.

Unearthly exclamations arose from the excited multitude; they might have been curses for aught we knew, and the terrific expressions of countenance, as revealed by starlight or the fitful flame of a paper lamp, made us think they were.

A lady of our company became alarmed; and well she might, for a couple of Greeks brushing against her, discovered that she had a watch in her pocket, and, as the speediest mode of securing the treasure, they actually tore from her nearly the whole skirt of her dress. Nervously did she cling to her husband; vigorously did he endeavor to protect her from harm, and loudly did he scream for Mustapha; but Mustapha, on account of the noise, heard him not; good, easy creature, he trudged along in blissful ignorance of the scenes that were being enacted in his rear, though he still mechanically grasped the hilt of his sword. At length, after frightening the Greeks by our calls for Mustapha, for they are afraid to injure any one who has Turkish protection, and succeeding, after many a hearty tug, in retaining a mere shred of the dress which happened to envelope the watch, the thieves slunk back into the crowd, and the most exciting, as well as the closing part of our adventures, was over.

With a little more pushing and elbowing we succeeded, ere long, in extricating ourselves from the throng, and in half an hour arrived home, thanking our stars that we had witnessed an "Illumination in honor of the Descent of the Koran," without paying, as a penalty, the forfeit of our lives.

CHAPTER XXV.

The Bairam—The Sultan Saluted by His Wives, and Complimented by the Dignitaries of the Land—A Brilliant Procession—Beautiful Picture—The *Corban Bairam*—Great Killing of Sheep.

On the first appearance of the new moon which succeeds the Ramazan, the Little *Bairam* commences. This is a season of uninterrupted pleasure and continues three days.

Universal hilarity reigns; and, with a zest augmented by the privations of the past few weeks, the Turk abandons himself to every rational enjoyment.

During this period we witnessed a grand ceremony, which annually occurs within the walls of the old Seraglio.

After the Sultan, within the Harem, had been saluted by his mother, his wives, and all his household, he seated himself near the grand entrance of the Seraglio; where, surrounded by his ministers, eunuchs, dwarfs, &c., he received the compliments and congratulations of the chief dignitaries of the empire.

The spectacle was indeed a magnificent one.

A brilliant procession was formed, composed of the *Sheikh Islam* or High Priest, the *Imaams* or Priests, the Cadis or religious Governors, Secretaries to Pashas, Capidgi Bashis, Kislar Aga or Chief of the Black Eunuchs, and led horses.

Music was discoursed by the Sultan's band as each dignitary approached, made his salaam, and then prostrated himself to kiss the hem of the Sultan's garment. The richness and variety of the Eastern costumes; the splendid caparisons of the spirited Arab horses, the very saddles being studded with diamonds and other precious gems; the dignified air of the distinguished personages; the peculiarly Oriental manner of their salutations and prostrations;—all combined to form a picture whose beauty was only surpassed by its singularity.

After the Sultan had been complimented by all the dignitaries, he proceeded with them, in grand procession, to the nearest mosque, where the illustrious party was soon absorbed in devotion to Allah and the Prophet.

The *Corban Bairam* is about two months after the

Little Bairam. This anniversary commemorates the flight of Mahomet, and is chiefly remarkable for the immense number of sheep that are sacrificed during its continuance. The roads leading into Constantinople are crowded with flocks of them, and everybody eats mutton.

CHAPTER XXVI.

TURKISH WEDDING.

Marriage negotiated by Female Relatives—The "Fair One" sought out by them—The Baths frequently Visited—Courting by Proxy—Falling in Love without seeing the Object loved—Handsome Presents to the Expected Bride—A mode of Popping the Question Expensive but Convenient to Modest Suitors—Assembling of Friends—The Lady escorted to the Bridegroom's House—Festivities—Tying of the Nuptial Knot—The Bride and Bridegroom unseen by each other before Marriage—Coquetting in the Bridal Chamber.

WHEN a young Turk desires to enter into a matrimonial alliance, he signifies his inclination to some elderly female relative, his aunt or mother, who then makes it her object to seek out some "fair one" whom she thinks would make an eligible match.

For this purpose she repairs frequently to the Baths, and carefully notes the form, the grace, the eyes, and the voice of the young females who there congregate daily to go through their ablutions.

Certainly no place could afford her better opportunities of acquainting herself with these matters.

When she has discovered a female (by thus frequenting the Baths and visiting around considerably among her friends, under the latter circumstances becoming acquainted with the lady's accomplishments, her skill in making conserves, embroidery, &c.), whom she considers suitable, in every respect, for the young man, she communicates to him what information she has been able to obtain concerning her.

If the young miss suits the old lady's fancy, she gives her son, or nephew, a glowing and highly wrought description of her charms; and, as he is willing to defer to the superior judgment of his mother, or aunt, in such matters, he speedily falls desperately in love with the fair incognita.

The old lady makes frequent visits to the relatives of the proposed bride, whom she informs of the young man's passion. If they treat her with much kindness, serve her with refreshments, &c., the supposition is, that the suit is favorably entertained.

After matters have thus progressed for awhile, the young man sends a present to the young lady,—a young gazelle, Cashmere shawl, Broussa silk, diamonds, &c.; and frequently, if he be very wealthy, he sends quite a profusion of these costly presents, several hamals and donkeys being employed to convey them to the lady's residence.

The acceptance of the present, or presents, by the young lady, is considered equivalent to an engagement.

At length, when the marriage is about to be consummated, the friends of the young man assemble at his house—the males in the *salamnik*, and the females in the *harem*—where they are served with refreshments. Soon the gentlemen proceed on horseback to the residence of the young lady, whom, she being seated on a donkey, and effectually screened from the observation of pedestrians, they escort to the young man's house. During this ceremony the party keep up a constant firing—every description of detonating weapon being brought into requisition that will add to the deafening clamor.

The young man meets his intended at the portal of his house, and helps her to alight,—the thick veil with which she is covered preventing him from seeing her face.

She is now conducted by the ladies of the house into the harem, where the festivities are kept up to a late hour. Music, dancing-girls, and refreshments here add to the pleasures of the occasion, whilst somewhat similar scenes are being enacted in the salamnik.

About nine or ten o'clock in the evening the nuptial knot is tied—the *Imaam*, or priest, placing himself in a short passage which leads between two rooms, respectively occupied by the bride and bridegroom, who neither see each other or the priest during the ceremony. That functionary now asks the bride if she will take this young man to be her husband, whether he be blind, halt, &c. She replies yes, three times.

They are now man and wife, though as yet they have not gazed on each other's features.

After this ceremony is concluded the festivities are resumed.

In the mean time the bride is escorted by her female friends to the bridal chamber, where she is seated on an ottoman, and left alone. Shortly after, the bridegroom makes his appearance. Discovering that his wife is still enveloped in her veil, he requests her to throw it aside, so that he can feast his eyes upon her beauty. This she coquettishly declines doing until he has become very earnest in his persuasions, when she discloses to him for the first time a view of her face.

After much persuasion on his part, and affected reluctance on hers, he at length succeeds in kissing her and——the curtain drops.

In the morning the bride's and bridegroom's relatives visit the bridal chamber, in accordance with an antiquated custom mentioned in Deuteronomy.

CHAPTER XXVII.

The Eastern War—Its Cause—American Sympathies—Actuating Motives of the Three Great Powers—Our Policy—Effects of the War upon Turkish Manners and Customs.

A WORD or two in reference to the Eastern War before we close.

The whole world is an eager spectator of that terrible conflict now waging between Turkey and the Great Colossus of the North.

The cause of this war is generally known. The Sultan has many thousand Greeks in his dominions, over whom, as Head of the Orthodox Faith, the Czar of Russia essayed to extend his Protectorate; making such demands as would, if granted, humiliate the Sultan, by depriving him of jurisdiction over a portion of his own subjects.

These demands were refused, and hence the outbreak of hostilities.

For months Turkey fought single-handed and alone against Russia; and every one will recollect the gallant manner in which Omer Pasha and his soldiers conducted themselves in the Danubian Provinces.

Then, owing to the causes of the war, Russia evidently being in the wrong; to the fact that Turkey was the weaker Power; to the chivalrous manner in which the Turks, under Omer Pasha, fought (they were a totally different set from those cowardly fellows in the Crimea), and to the circumstance that Turkey had sheltered the oppressed Hungarians, the sympathies of America were mostly enlisted in her behalf.

But so soon as England and France became arrayed against Russia, nominally to protect Turkey against the aggressions of the Czar, nominally as the champions of the weak against the strong, but really for their own self-agrandizement and to maintain the political equilibrium in Europe, the sympathies of our countrymen assumed pretty much the character of those felt by the woman who, when witnessing a desperate struggle between her husband and a bear, declared that "it was the first fight she ever saw that she didn't care which whipped."

Neither England nor France care a picayune for Turkey, save it be to dismember and divide her empire between them; and as Russia is animated by equally amiable and disinterested motives, the result of the war, so far as these three great Powers are concerned, cannot be a matter of any great moment to us Republicans.

As a Nation, our only proper and politic position in the matter is a rigidly neutral one; and we should congratulate ourselves that our beloved country is so far removed from those discordant elements which are now agitating the Old World to its very base.

Whether Constantinople will pass into the hands of the English or French, or whether Alexander II. will be triumphant, we are unable to divine; but should neither of these events transpire, it cannot be doubted that the effect of the war, arising from the constant intercommunication existing between the Turks, and the English and French officers and soldiers, and the powerfully civilizing influence naturally originating from an alliance with two such Powers as England and France, will be, a gradual but perceptible change in those distinctive Oriental features of the Turks which we have feebly attempted to portray.

CHAPTER XXVIII.

HOMEWARD BOUND.

Leave Constantinople—Malta—Sicily—A Gale between Scylla and Charybdis—Pompeii—Rome—Its Antiquities—Driven into Elba by a Storm—Florence—Genoa—Return to Paris—Our Route—Home Again—Conclusion.

We bade adieu to Constantinople on the 6th of November, 1852, and in six days arrived at Malta; *en route* we stopped at Smyrna and the Greek island of Syra.

Most agreeable were the ten days we spent on the Island of Malta, wandering through the Botanic Garden of Floriana; exploring the Catacombs, near Citta-Vecchia and the Grotto of St. Paul; admiring the rich mosaics and magnificent sepulchral monuments of the Church of St. John, the patron of the Order of the Knights of Malta; the Palace of the Grand Master, which contains so many noble relics of that illustrious Order, &c.

We left Malta at night, and the next morning were among the antiquities of Syracuse; the same day, threading the lava streets of Catania, and gazing on Etna in eruption.

The following morning, we lay in the lovely harbor of Messina; the city, backed by noble hills, lying amphitheatrically around us.

Between Scylla and Charybdis, on our way to Naples, we experienced a most dreadful gale. The wind appeared to blow from the four quarters of heaven; the waters were lashed into a fury; the boat tossed and lurched terribly, changing our expressions of admiration in regard to the charming scenery along the Sicilian coast, into imprecations against the sea, and reflections upon the shipwrecks of the ancients in that dangerous pass.

We made a brief sojourn in Naples; and over the spray-washed road of Castelmaré, with Vesuvius in full view all the time, we drove to ancient Pompeii; whose palaces, forums, baths, and public squares, mosaics, and frescoes, are now, after having undisturbedly reposed under the lava and ashes of the neighboring volcano for eighteen centuries, being developed by the pickaxe and the spade.

Two days in our carriage, a night at Mola de

Gaeta, and one at Terracina, and our eyes are feasting upon the splendid ruins of ancient Rome, now slumbering, in solemn grandeur, around the modern city.

There is the Coliseum, which still stands high and bold, despite the ravages of time, and its having been despoiled of sufficient material to construct two or three palaces; unfractured columns and obelisks of the olden time still stand in the public squares; the Roman cardinals' carriages rattle under the arches of Constantine, Titus, and of Trajan, now, as did the heavy chariots in the days of the Consuls, when bearing the laurel-crowned victors; still stands in a modest site, the little temple of Vesta, where, in days of yore, vigils were kept over the sacred flame; and the Catholic devotee bows down to images of saints and holy crucifixes in the grand old Pantheon, the best preserved of all the antiquities in Rome.

Let us stand on the palace of the Cæsars, itself a mass of majestic ruins, overgrown by moss and ivy, and gaze upon those half-standing, half-crumbling temples, baths, amphitheatres, palaces, &c., whose noble relics attest their former splendor. Near us are all the famous structures that adorned the Capitoline Hill; far over the Campagna rises mound after mound, all the sites of noble piles that skirted the Appian Way. And we can also trace the ancient wall of Rome, and broken lines of Roman aqueducts.

But St. Peter's has been visited; the Pope seen; we have dwelt in rapture upon the wondrous productions of the chisel and the brush, which grace the galleries of the Eternal City; in her thronged streets we have noticed the striking contrast between regal state and ecclesiastical domination on the one hand, and abject poverty and superstition on the other; and with the consolatory thought that we were hurrying to a land the spirit of whose institutions and government is adverse to a union of the spiritual and temporal, we bade adieu to Rome, and in a day or two, northward steering, were sailing over the blue waters of the Mediterranean.

A storm at night gave us a very disagreeable tossing; made us all desperately sea-sick; but by driving us into the port of Elba, afforded us the unanticipated pleasure of wandering through the fortifications of that celebrated isle.

We visited Leghorn, Pisa, and then the beautiful Florence. Oh, who could faithfully portray the beauty of the Valley of the Arno; or thee, Florence, with thy Boboli Gardens, thy Cascine, Duomo, Palazzo

Vecchia, thy Pitti Palace, and thy rich treasures of old paintings and statues?

A view from the top of the Leaning Tower of Pisa; a brief sojourn in Leghorn; a pleasant little sea-voyage; and we were traversing the gorgeous palaces and churches of Genoa.

The route from Marseilles to Lyons, and from thence to Paris in the coupé of a diligence, was rather tedious, and rejoiced were we when we arrived in the French metropolis; where, from the front windows of our hotel, we could look right out upon the lovely garden of Les Tuileries.

We had been in Paris before, on our way to Constantinople. Our route was from Paris to Strasburg on the Rhine, from thence to Basle, Lucerne, and over the Alps to Milan, Padua, Verona, Venice, Trieste, &c.

Homeward bound, we went to Calais; recrossed the English Channel; and, in the ill-fated Arctic, after a boisterous voyage of fifteen days, arrived in "our own, our native land."

We now close, by again intimating that the reason why we have purposely avoided giving an account of our travels in civilized Europe, is attributable to the fact, that that portion of the world is written and rewritten upon to such a degree, that the subject is almost exhausted, and is, moreover, less interesting, because not so novel, as the matters we have mainly devoted our remarks to.

Our object has been simply to give the reader an idea of Oriental Life; of those things which do not come under the observation of the major portion of those who cross the ocean; and if, here and there, we have afforded any entertainment, or furnished any new items of information, we will feel more than compensated for our pains.

There are many other Oriental matters which we might speak of; and should this little book meet with popular favor, we will be encouraged to make them the subjects of a larger and more complete volume.

THE END.

THE CHRISTIAN FAMILY LIBRARY.

THE WOMEN OF THE OLD AND NEW TESTAMENT.

SCENES IN THE LIFE OF THE SAVIOUR.

SCENES IN THE LIVES OF THE PATRIARCHS AND PROPHETS.

SCENES IN THE LIVES OF THE APOSTLES.

Neat 12mo. Volumes, with Illustrations. Price per volume, in Cloth, Plain Edges, Gilt Backs, 75 cents. Full Gilt Edges, $1 00. In Setts, Cloth, Plain, $3 00. In Full Gilt, $4 00.

THE CHESTERFIELDIAN LIBRARY.

MANUALS FOR THE POCKET OR CENTRE-TABLE.

THE YOUNG HUSBAND,

A MANUAL OF THE DUTIES, MORAL, RELIGIOUS, AND DOMESTIC, IMPOSED BY THE RELATIONS OF MARRIED LIFE.

THE YOUNG WIFE,

A MANUAL OF MORAL, RELIGIOUS, AND DOMESTIC DUTIES,

BEING A COMPANION TO "THE YOUNG HUSBAND."

ETIQUETTE FOR GENTLEMEN,

OR, SHORT RULES AND REFLECTIONS FOR CONDUCT IN SOCIETY.

ETIQUETTE FOR LADIES,

WITH HINTS ON THE PRESERVATION, IMPROVEMENT, ETC., OF FEMALE BEAUTY.

THE HAND-BOOK OF ETIQUETTE,

OR CANONS OF GOOD BREEDING.

BY THE AUTHOR OF "ETIQUETTE FOR GENTLEMEN."

JOHNSON'S POCKET DICTIONARY.

A NEW AND REVISED EDITION. WITH A PORTRAIT OF THE AUTHOR.

Each volume neatly bound in Cloth, Gilt Backs, with an Illuminated Frontispiece. Price 38 cents, or in Full Gilt, 50 cents. In Setts, Cloth, Plain, $2 25; Full Gilt, $3 00.

AN ILLUSTRATED LIFE OF MARTIN LUTHER,

THE GREAT GERMAN REFORMER. With a Sketch of the Reformation in Germany. Edited, with an Introduction, by the REV. THEOPHILUS STORK, D.D., late Pastor of St. Mark's Luthern Church, Philadelphia. Beautifully ILLUSTRATED by sixteen designs, printed on fine paper. A handsome octavo volume.

Price, in cloth, gilt backs, - - - - - $2 00
full gilt, - - - - - - 2 50
In embossed leather, marble edges, gilt backs, &c., 2 25

The world owes much to Luther, and the Reformation of which he was the prominent leader, and nothing, save the pure, simple word of God, will do more towards securing the prevalence and perpetuating the influence of the principles of religious liberty for which he and the other Reformers contended, than the circulation of a book in which the mental processes by which he arrived at his conclusions, are set forth. We can safely recommend this book as one that is worthy of a place in every dwelling, and we hope its circulation may be as wide as its merits are deserving.—*Evangelical Magazine.*

THE LIFE OF PHILIP MELANCHTHON,

THE FRIEND AND COMPANION OF LUTHER, According to his Inner and Outer Life. Translated from the German of Charles Frederick Ledderhose, by the REV. G. F. KROTEL, Pastor of the Trinity Lutheran Church, Lancaster, Pa. With a PORTRAIT of Melanchthon. In one Volume, 12mo. **Price $1 00.**

THE PARABLES OF FRED'K ADOLPHUS KRUMMACHER.

From the seventh German edition. Elegantly ILLUSTRATED by Twenty-six Original Designs, beautifully printed on fine paper. A handsome demy octavo volume.

Elegantly bound in cloth, gilt backs, - - - Price $1 75
.. .. full gilt sides, backs and edges, 2 50
.. .. Turkey morocco, antique, - 4 00

The simple and Christian parables of Krummacher, chiefly the productions of his younger years, have acquired a wide popularity, and have long afforded a fund on which our periodicals have freely drawn. In their collected form they have passed through various editions in Germany, but we doubt whether any of them have been so tasteful and beautiful in all their appliances as the one before us. The typography is very chaste, and the illustrations neat and appropriate.—*Presbyterian.*

THE CHRISTIAN'S DAILY DELIGHT.

A SACRED GARLAND, CULLED FROM ENGLISH AND AMERICAN POETS. Beautifully ILLUSTRATED by Eight Engravings on Steel.

In one volume, demy, octavo, cloth, gilt backs, - Price $1 50
.. .. full gilt sides, backs and edges, 2 25

In this attractive volume we find much to please the eye; but the most valuable recommendation of the work is found in the lessons of piety, virtue, morality, and mercy, which are thrown together in this many-coloured garland of poetic flowers.—*Episcopal Recorder.*

The Rev. John Cumming's Works.

UNIFORM EDITION.

Price 75 cents per Volume, and sent by mail, free of postage, upon receipt of this amount by the Publishers.

CUMMING'S APOCALYPTIC SKETCHES;

OR, LECTURES ON THE BOOK OF REVELATION.

One Volume, 12mo. Cloth.

CUMMING'S APOCALYPTIC SKETCHES.

SECOND SERIES. One Volume, 12mo. Cloth.

CUMMING'S LECTURES ON THE SEVEN CHURCHES.

One Volume, 12mo. Cloth.

CUMMING'S LECTURES ON OUR LORD'S MIRACLES.

One Volume, 12mo. Cloth.

CUMMING'S LECTURES ON THE PARABLES.

One Volume. 12mo. Cloth.

CUMMING'S PROPHETIC STUDIES;

OR, LECTURES ON THE BOOK OF DANIEL.

One Volume, 12mo. Cloth.

CUMMING'S MINOR WORKS. First Series.

One Volume, 12mo. Cloth. This Volume contains the following:

THE FINGER OF GOD, CHRIST OUR PASSOVER, THE COMFORTER.

Which are all bound and sold separately. Price 38 cents.

CUMMING'S MINOR WORKS. Second Series.

One Volume, 12mo. Cloth. This Volume contains the following:

A MESSAGE FROM GOD, THE GREAT SACRIFICE, AND CHRIST RECEIVING SINNERS.

Which are also bound and sold separately. Price 38 cents.

The Rev. John Cumming, D.D., is now the great pulpit orator of London, as Edward Irving was some twenty years since. But very different is the Doctor to that strange, wonderfully eloquent, but erratic man. There could not by possibility be a greater contrast. The one all fire, enthusiasm, and semi-madness; the other a man of chastened energy and convincing calmness. The one like a meteor, flashing across a troubled sky, and then vanishing suddenly in the darkness; the other like a silver star, shining serenely, and illuminating our pathway with its steady ray. He is looked upon as the great champion of Protestantism in its purest form.

His great work on the "Apocalypse," upon which his high reputation as a writer rests, having already reached its fifteenth edition in England, while his "Lectures on the Miracles," and those on "Daniel," have passed through six editions of 1000 copies each, and his "Lectures on the Parables" through four editions, all within a comparatively short time.

KURTEN'S ART OF MANUFACTURING SOAPS.

INCLUDING THE MOST RECENT DISCOVERIES. Embracing the best methods for making all kinds of HARD, SOFT, and TOILET SOAPS; also OLIVE OIL SOAP, and others necessary in the Preparation of Cloths. With Receipts for making TRANSPARENT and CAMPHINE OIL CANDLES. By PHILIP KURTEN, Practical Soap and Candle Manufacturer. In one vol., 12mo. Price $1 00.

PIGGOTT ON COPPER MINING AND COPPER ORE.

Containing a full description of some of the principal Copper Mines of the United States, the Art of Mining, the Mode of Preparing the Ore for Market, &c. &c. By A. SNOWDEN PIGGOTT, M. D., Practical Chemist. In one volume, 12mo. Price $1 00.

OVERMAN'S PRACTICAL MINERALOGY, ASSAYING, AND MINING.

With a Description of the Useful Minerals, and Instructions for Assaying and Mining, according to the Simplest Methods. By FREDERICK OVERMAN, Mining Engineer, &c. Third Edition. In one volume, 12mo. Price 75 cents.

WRIGHT'S AMERICAN RECEIPT BOOK,

Containing over 3000 Receipts, in all the Useful and Domestic Arts; including Confectionery, Distilling, Perfumery, Chemicals, Varnishes, Dyeing, Agriculture, &c. &c. In one volume. Price $1 00.

MORFIT'S MANURES,

Their Composition, Preparation, and Action upon Soils, with the Quantities to be applied. A much-needed Manual for the Farmer. By CAMPBELL MORFIT, Practical and Analytical Chemist. Price only 25 cents.

MORFIT'S PHARMACEUTICAL MANUAL.

CHEMICAL AND PHARMACEUTICAL MANIPULATIONS. A Manual of the Mechanical and Chemico-Mechanical Operations of the Laboratory. By C. MORFIT, assisted by Alex. Muckle. One vol., 8vo., with nearly 500 ILLUSTRATIONS. Price $2 00.

NOAD'S CHEMICAL ANALYSIS,

QUALITATIVE AND QUANTITATIVE. By HENRY M. NOAD, Lecturer on Chemistry at St. George's Hospital, author of "Lectures on Electricity," "Lectures on Chemistry," &c. &c. With numerous additions by Campbell Morfit, Practical and Analytical Chemist, author of "Chemical and Pharmaceutical Manipulations," &c. With ILLUSTRATIONS. One vol., 8vo. Price $2 00.

NEW DICTIONARIES.

WALKER'S RHYMING DICTIONARY:

A Rhyming, Spelling, and Pronouncing Dictionary of the English Language---in which

I. The whole Language is arranged according to its terminations.

II. Every Word is explained and divided into Syllables exactly as pronounced.

III. Multitudes of Words liable to a double pronunciation are fixed in their true sound by a rhyme.

IV. Many of the most difficult Words are rendered easy to be pronounced by being classed according to their endings.

V. Numerous classes of Words are ascertained in their pronunciation, by distinguishing them into perfect, nearly perfect, and allowable Rhymes.

To which is prefixed a copious introduction to the various uses of the work, with critical and practical observations on Orthography, Syllabication, Pronunciation, and Rhyme; and, for the purpose of Poetry, is added an Index of Allowable Rhymes, with authorities for their usage from our best Poets.

BY J. WALKER.

One vol. 12mo. Price $1 25.

Here is a book that the young poet—and the old one, too, perhaps—will find one of his most valuable assistants. It will not furnish him with inspiration, but it will readily furnish him with rhymes, which are often the best aids in the flow of inspiration. Many a sublime thought or pretty fancy has been irretrievably lost while the poet was scratching his head for a word with the proper jingle. This dictionary removes all these troubles, since it furnishes every word in the language according to its termination. In all this there is no child's play, for such a work has its value and its dignity, and its value is above the mere manufacture of couplets. The endorsement of Walker to the system given in his work would alone raise it above ridicule, even if it had not been for years considered a work of real value by the best minds in England and this country. Walker's system of orthography and pronunciation continues to be the standard among all our best writers, and these are fully developed in this dictionary. His introduction contains an invaluable treatise on the construction of our language. The work is very well printed and bound.—*Bulletin.*

RAWSON'S NEW DICTIONARY OF SYNONYMES:

A Dictionary of the Synonymical Terms of the English Language.

BY THE REV. JAMES RAWSON.

A neat 12mo. Volume. Price 63 cents.

Of the various books of English Synonymes that have been published, none is at once so compact, comprehensive, clear, and correct as this one. The number of synonymical terms is larger than any previous work contains, and there is nothing superfluous—no unnecessary remarks, which are more calculated to bewilder than to inform. It will make an admirable desk companion for the man of letters.—*Evening Bulletin.*

JOHNSON'S POCKET DICTIONARY.

DIAMOND EDITION.

32mo. Cloth,....................................38 cents.
" Embossed gilt....................................50 "
" Tucks gilt edges....................................63 "

This edition has been greatly improved by the addition of some thousand words and technical terms, the accentuation corrected according to the most approved mode of pronunciation, together with a concise classical mythology, a list of men of learning and genius, phrases from various languages, and a biographical table of distinguished deceased Americans, and a portrait of Dr. Johnson

LINDSAY AND BLAKISTON

PUBLISH

A MANUAL OF SACRED HISTORY;

OR,

A GUIDE TO THE UNDERSTANDING

Of the Divine Plan of Salvation

ACCORDING TO ITS HISTORICAL DEVELOPMENT.

BY

JOHN HENRY KURTZ, D.D.,

PROFESSOR OF CHURCH HISTORY IN THE UNIVERSITY OF DORPAT, ETC.

TRANSLATED FROM THE SIXTH GERMAN EDITION,

BY

CHARLES F. SCHAEFFER, D.D.,

OPINIONS OF THE PRESS.

"A very comprehensive, accurate, and methodical digest of the Sacred History — done with genuine thoroughness and scholarship. There is nothing among our manuals of Biblical History that corresponds with this. It is simple in style, and orthodox in sentiment."—*N. Y. Evangelist.*

"The Observations (introduced by the author) are replete with the results of extensive research—meeting objections and cavils, solving difficulties, explaining obscure passages, reconciling apparent discrepancies, pointing out connectious, exposing and rectifying errors, unfolding the nature and design of sacred institutions and ordinances, and showing the relation of events, persons, institutions and prophecies, to the great central fact and theme of Scripture, man's redemption through the incarnate Son." — *Evangelical Review, April,* 1855.

"This is the best book of the kind we have ever examined, and one of the best translations from German into English we have ever seen. The author makes no parade of learning in his book, but his exegetical statements are evidently founded on the most careful, thorough, and extensive study, and can generally be relied upon as among the best results, the most surely ascertained conclusions of modern philological investigation. We by no means hold ourselves responsible for every sentiment in the book, but we cordially recommend it to every minister, to every Sunday school teacher, to every parent, and to every intelligent layman, as a safe and exceedingly instructive guide, through the entire Bible history, the Old Testament and the New. It is a book which actually accomplishes more than its title promises," &c. &c.—(*Andover*) *Bibliotheca Sacra, April,* 1855.

Notices by the Press of Kurtz's Sacred History,

PUBLISHED BY LINDSAY AND BLAKISTON, PHILADELPHIA.

Dr. J. H. KURTZ's Manual of Sacred History is the production of a very able and pious divine of our church in Europe. The author is particularly distinguished for his learning, his orthodoxy, his liberality, his piety, and his originality. He writes with great clearness and condensation, and presents in a brief compass a large amount of matter. His various works, and particularly his Histories, have received the highest endorsement abroad in their popularity and multiplied editions, and are commended in the strongest terms by the most eminent divines. Guericke, Bruno Lindner, and Rudelbach, laud his Histories in the strongest terms, and the Evangelical Review,* in the United States, has furnished evidence of his great merits from authentic sources. The admirable Manual of Sacred History, translated by Dr. Schaeffer, (and, having examined some parts of the translation, we may say *well* translated,) will constitute a rich contribution to our theological literature. Having encouraged the translator to undertake the work, we are the more free to express our high opinion of it, and the fidelity with which it has been executed. We hope this will be the forerunner of other translations of works of the author.

C. P. KRAUTH,

Professor of Sac. Phil. Church Hist. and Past. Theol.. Gettysburg, Pa.

Sept. 16, 1854.

The *Sacred History* of Dr. J. H. Kurtz, does not belong to the ordinary class of historic Manuals, with which the literature of Germany abounds. On the contrary, after considerable acquaintance with it, we hesitate not to pronounce it a production of very superior merit in its department, possessed of high literary and theological excellence. Its style is pure and perspicuous, its divisions are natural and appropriate, and the grouping of events felicitous and impressive. Without assenting to every sentiment of the author, we cordially recommend his work to the patronage of the Christian public, and consider Dr. Schaeffer as entitled to the gratitude of the church, for presenting this Manual to the English public in so accurate and excellent a translation.

S. S. SCHMUCKER,

Professor of Didactic, Polemic and Homiletic Theology, in Theol. Sem. of Gettysburg.

Sept. 17, 1854.

I know of no work in the English or German language which gives, in so short a compass, so full and clear an account of the gradual development of the divine plan of salvation, from the fall of man to the resurrection of Christ and the founding of the apostolic church, and which is, at the same time, so sound in sentiment, so evangelical in tone, and, without being superficial, so well adapted for popular use, as the "Manual of Sacred History," by Dr. J. H. Kurtz. The translation of the Rev. Dr. Charles F. Schaeffer seems to me, as far as I have examined it, to do full justice to the German original, as well as to the English idiom.

PHILIP SCHAFF,

Prof. of Ch. Hist., &c.

Mercersburg, Pa., Jan. 31, 1855.

* July, 1853, p. 138.

Notices by the Press of Kurtz's Sacred History,

PUBLISHED BY LINDSAY AND BLAKISTON, PHILADELPHIA.

" * * * It would seem that the author of this work is one of that class of individuals on whom God has bestowed ten talents. * * * The author is a methodical thinker; he narrates in the most beautiful language and in great clearness, though in a condensed form. * * * The translator has placed in the sacred historical library a work of rare merit."—*Easton Whig, of Jan.* 17, 1855.

"The author's remarkable genius and vast attainments have already given him a place among the greatest lights in theology and history on the continent of Europe. The present work * * * requires to be thoroughly examined in order to a full appreciation of its highly evangelical type, of its lucid arrangement, of its felicitous selection of historical events, of the harmony of the various parts, and the bearing of the whole upon one glorious consummation. * * There are few minds, if any, that have thought so extensively or so profoundly on the subjects of which it treats, that they may not be instructed by it. Dr. Schaeffer has performed his work as translator in a manner that fully satisfies those who are most competent to judge of the merits of the translation."—*Albany Argus, of Jan.* 24, 1855.

"We cannot but regard this work as a valuable aid to our own students and instructors, from its clear and pregnant summary of facts, its lively and original suggestions, and its constant exhibition of unity in all God's plans and dispensations, of which even the most pious and attentive readers of the Bible are too much accustomed to lose sight.

"This book is, according to the Lutheran standard, thoroughly orthodox in matters of doctrine, and is more thoroughly religious in spirit than any similar German work with which we are acquainted.

"The English translation is, in our opinion, highly creditable to its author; not only accurate, so far as we have yet had time to judge it, but less disfigured by undue adherence to German idiom, by awkward stiffness, and by weak verbosity, than any version we have recently examined."—*Biblical Repertory and Princeton Review, of Jan.* 1855.

"It is a work of great value, not only on account of its literary excellence, and the profound theological knowledge displayed in it, but especially as supplying a great want in a clear, simple, and thorough explanation of all the difficult points and obscure questions both as to doctrine and ecclesiastical polity in the Bible.

"All who are desirous of a thorough understanding of Bible history should possess themselves of this learned and interesting work."—*Eastonian, of Jan.* 27, 1855.

Notices by the Press of Kurtz's Sacred History,

PUBLISHED BY LINDSAY AND BLAKISTON, PHILADELPHIA.

"This volume deserves to be in every family; all may read and study it with profit. It is well adapted for schools and seminaries of learning and theology. * * We are pleased to learn that arrangements have been already made for its immediate introduction into Esther Female Institute and Capital University. We know of no work in any language, in all the bounds of sacred literature, calculated to exert a more wholesome and beneficial influence in the cause of Christ, than this work."—*Lutheran Standard, (Columbus, O.) of Jan.* 26, 1855.

"* * * The present volume treats of the subject of Sacred History on a novel plan. It furnishes a suggestive comment on the incidents recorded in the Bible, considered as illustrations of the divine purpose in the salvation of man. The style is clear, compact, and forcible, presenting a mass of weighty thoughts, in simple and appropriate language."—*N. Y. Tribune, of Jan.* 5, 1855.

"* * An important addition to the line of text-books. The plan of the work is as novel as it is happy. * * * Like all other of the recent German theological and metaphysical works, the analytical arrangement is exquisitely delicate and minute, perhaps too much so; and the amount of valuable historical material as well as of doctrinal exposition it contains, bears a proportion to the amount of space which those who are accustomed to our own looser method of composition may well welcome."—*Episcopal Recorder.*

"The arrangement is admirable, the explanatory remarks are instructive, and the whole work one of marked ability." * * —*Baltimore (Baptist) True Union.*

"All classes of readers may study it with advantage."—*N. Y. Commercial.*

"An admirable volume. Its literary and theological merits are of a high order, and entitle it to a wide circulation among the lovers of a religious literature. The translator has faithfully executed his task."—*Christian Chronicle.*

"It is a work of great value as a text-book for Bible classes and schools, and which may be made extensively useful in a family."—*(Boston) Daily Evening Traveller.*

"It is considered a profound, learned, and thoroughly Protestant work. * * The translation is made from the sixth German edition, and will be of use to theologians, as we understand there has never been one issued in this country." —*Even. Bulletin, (Phil.) of Jan.* 27, 1855.

www.ingramcontent.com/pod-product-compliance
Lightning Source LLC
LaVergne TN
LVHW011221110826
845150LV00006B/1495

* 9 7 8 1 4 2 5 5 1 5 9 3 5 *